C000179671

The Diary of

The Reverend Matthew Paterson

Hospital Chaplain
Glasgow Royal Infirmary 1878-1881

Adam Plenderleith
Neil E Allison

Copyright © Adam Plenderleith

All rights reserved. No part of this publication may be
reproduced, stored in a retrieval system, or
transmitted, in any form or by means,
electronic, mechanical, photocopying, recording
or otherwise, without the prior written permission of the copyright holder.

First Edition: 2017

Published by Scottish History 2017 Project

ISBN 978-1-9998700-4-1

Printed in Great Britain by

Biddles Books Limited, King's Lynn, Norfolk

ACKNOWLEDGEMENTS

Alistair Tough NHSGGC Archivist for awakening me to a new world of NHS GGC Archives, **John Stuart** Chief Nurse NHS Greater Glasgow & Clyde for his enthusiastic support; **Ruth Allison** for sharing helpful research and reading through parts of the manuscript making helpful corrections; **David Stowe** for providing additional information. **Godfrey Warren** for his wisdom and encouragement. And finally my wife **Hilary** for her love, patience and understanding without whom nothing would have been completed.

with richest Blessings

Adam

12/11/17

CONTRIBUTORS

Rev. Adam Plenderleith is a Baptist Minister who has served as both church pastor and hospital chaplain for the past 15 years. Prior to his ordination in Baptist Ministry he worked for the NHS gaining qualifications in General Nursing, Psychiatric Nursing and Health Visiting. Since 2011 he has been a hospital chaplain at Glasgow Royal Infirmary and had the privilege of serving on the committee of the Dorcas Society. It was during his time at Glasgow Royal Infirmary that he came across the diary of the Reverend Matthew Paterson.

Rev. Dr Neil E Allison FSA Scot is a Baptist Minister who has served as both a church pastor and military chaplain over the past 24 years. Since 2006 he was appointed as the Official historian to the United Navy, Army and Air Force Board, and is the founder of the United Board History Project. In 2013 he was appointed an External Senior Lecturer in Chaplaincy and Pastoral Studies for North West University South Africa and Greenwich School of Theology, London. In 2015 he was appointed a post-doctoral Research Fellow of the Highland Theological College, University of the Highlands and Islands. His area of research: "The Function and Role of Chaplains during the Wars of the Three Kingdoms (1642-1660)." In 2017 he was made a Fellow of the Royal Society of Antiquaries Scotland.

PREFACE

This document, a diary of Rev Matthew Paterson who is the main Chaplain in Glasgow Royal Infirmary, runs from June 1878 until the end of 1881 and is the record of zealous spiritual work in a very busy hospital in an industrial city. Patients come from a fairly wide area, with different illnesses, and after severe accidents. Paterson is an assiduous ward visitor, conducts well-attended services each Sunday and from time to time visits the nearby Poorhouse. So much of what he does resonates with present day experience. He attends emergencies, and visits several wards each day. He discovers many patients and staff searching for spiritual help, and sometimes staff are less than helpful and subsequently apologise, blaming tiredness. Eminent clergy occasionally visit, and he names Dr Marshall Lang, father of a future Archbishop of Canterbury. Some well-meaning visitors speak in wards and frighten patients with alarming messages, and I am reminded that until fairly recently groups from evangelical churches would 'have a ward in the Infirmary.'

But the differences are more apparent. There are many entries which highlight the widespread poverty in the West of Scotland at the time. Paterson is quite unapologetic about preaching in the wards, and preaching for a verdict. He does not always wait to be invited to speak of spiritual matters, but goes straight to the point. Unsurprisingly he has varied reactions, especially from Roman Catholic patients, some of whom he views as potential converts, and others who are vocally opposed to him. Some indifferent patients who do not wish to listen to him he threatens with 'the rules' and that definitely places him within the management of the institution. Staff, including leading doctors, are generally supportive and noted as attending Sunday services, and he is obviously highly regarded. Christian festivals which are so prominent now are quite ignored. Christmas is just another day of visiting and preaching. There are a few accounts of deathbed conversions, and patients usually have some understanding of the Christian faith, whereas now that cannot be assumed.

As a portrait of a busy chaplain's work in an era which seems sometimes to have vanished and which yet has echoes today this is an invaluable document, and may be commended to today's Healthcare chaplains as a sort of mirror to their work and outlook.

Rev Dr Derek Murray

President Scottish Church History Society 2007-1010 & Hospice Chaplain

INTRODUCTION

The Royal Infirmary was founded on need. The need was for Glasgow to provide a hospital to care for its burgeoning population drawn to Glasgow by expanding trade of the Industrial Revolution. Church, Town and University recognised the problem and worked closely together to find a solution. The generosity of public minded citizens of all backgrounds enabled the entire development of the infirmary to be funded by charitable donations.[1]

George Jardine, Logic Lecturer at the Glasgow University, was the inspiration behind the founding of the hospital. In August 1791 a committee of subscribers was formed and Jardine was elected Secretary to organise the founding of a hospital for the "Relief of the Indigent Persons labouring under Poverty and Disease."[2] This had become an urgent requirement because of the "increased population of the Classes of Manufacture and labours of every kind, who are most likely to require charitable assistance."[3] It was to be a 'Voluntary Hospital' which depended on the support and goodwill of subscribers and Medical and Surgical staff who took no salary. The patients themselves were not charged for the cost of the hospital bed and treatment. "The rationale behind this new attitude to health care provision lay in the growing concern of the mercantilist circles that the prosperity of the nation was dependent upon the size and health of the population."[4]

Christian influence had a marked presence in the hospital. One faith inspired initiative was the founding of 'The Dorcas Society'[5] in 1863 by a

---

1 A. Ross Lorimer in *The Royal:The History of the Glasgow Royal Infirmary: 1794-1994*, (Glasgow: Glasgow Royal Infirmary NHS Trust, 1994), p.107
2 Jacqueline Jenkinson; Michael Moss; Iain Russell *The Royal: The History of the Glasgow Royal Infirmary 1794-1994*, (Glasgow: Glasgow Royal Infirmary NHS Trust,1994), p.11
3 *Glasgow Royal Infirmary*, p.11
4 *Glasgow Royal Infirmary*, p.13
5 See https://dorcasgri.worldpress.com; *Glasgow Royal Infirmary*, p p.118-119

Miss Clugston. She was moved by the poverty of the poor patients whose clothes were often threadbare and lice ridden. Inspired by the story of Dorcas in Acts 9:36-43 she collected clothes from the better off to give to the patients when they left hospital which gave them a better chance of staying well because they were now warm and better able to withstand the withering Scottish weather especially during the winter. A few years later the Society worked to provide an 'Invalid chair' for every ward.[6] But at the Societies heart was that the living God, in Christ, could meet the needs of the patient and to that end "Lady volunteers visited the wards to lead prayers and bible readings, and offer spiritual comfort to the elderly and lonely."[7]

From its opening on 8 December 1794[8] to the time this diary was written, 1878 to 1881, there had been significant developments to the fabric of the hospital as well as staff training and practice enabling the hospital to deal with numbers of patients the founders would have found hard to imagine. Yet in spite of all the developments and improvements "suppurative and putrefactive conditions were endemic."[9] How infection crossed from one patient to another was little understood. Surgeons would operate in dirty gowns and other staff would carry infection from one patient to other. Mortality from infection was always high.

The arrival of a young Surgeon Joseph Lister (1827-1912)[10] in August 1861 would initiate and lead the charge against infection with carbolic acid and the application of effective nursing cleansing management. Nursing was beginning to become progressively respected, largely because of the work of Florence Nightingale (1820-1910) and her nurses. Certainly Lister recognised their worth and noted that: "I was fortunate to have excellent nurses from the commencement of my connextion (*sic*) with the infirmary".[11]

---

6   *Glasgow Royal Infirmary*, p.119
7   *Glasgow Royal Infirmary*, p.119
8   *Glasgow Royal Infirmary*, p.21
9   *Glasgow Royal Infirmary*, p.107
10 *Glasgow Royal Infirmary*, p.108-114
11 *Glasgow Royal Infirmary*, p.113

The hospital continued to develop and expand as additional staff were appointed. From 1861 to 1892 "the standards of comfort and care offered to patients at the Royal improved almost beyond recognition."[12] This was because improvements in staff discipline and hygiene created a more sterile environment for the better trained Doctors and nurses to work within.

During this period of history religion and particularly Christianity were important to most of the population and therefore of interest to the media. In such a climate the significant influx of Irish Roman Catholic immigrants into largely Protestant Glasgow caused regular eruptions of sectarian feeling, with occasional rioting fuelled by events in Ireland.

In 1877 the loss of financial support became a real concern to the Managers. On the 13 September a letter was published in the *Daily Mail* that responding to an article in the *Belfast News* which alleged that "the majority of nurses at the Royal were Catholics; and they burned Protestant religious literature; actively attempted to convert patients to Catholicism; and favoured Catholics when choosing those to be sent to convalescent homes."[13] After a significant investigation, to answer concerns raised by the West of Scotland Protestant Association (WSPA) into the accusation that the hospital favoured Roman Catholics, it was decided that there was no truth in the accusations. However Paterson has two diary entries referring to whole batches of literature going missing which suggests that at least one concern had some basis in fact. This incident led at least one significant benefactor withdrawing his financial support[14] but the Royal remained established through another crisis.

But what do we know of the writer of this diary? Very little personal information is recorded in its pages, but further research has uncovered the following information. Mr Matthew Paterson was born in or around 1839 in Lanarkshire. He married Sarah Graham, from Hutchesontown, Glasgow, on 31 December 1862 and they had four children. Their first son, Matthew, was born on 16 November 1863 in Old Luce, Wigtown, Dumfriesshire. He was followed by a younger brother and two sisters all

---

12 *Glasgow Royal Infirmary*, p.139
13 *Glasgow Royal Infirmary*, p.122
14 *Glasgow Royal Infirmary*, pp.121-123

of whom were born in St Andrews in Fife: Robert Alexander born on 16 March 1866; Mary Bella born on 11 August 1868 and Elizabeth Graham born on 2 July 1871.[15]

Paterson worked for nine years in St Andrews as a missionary under the auspices of the Scottish Coast Mission. From this ministry he was "unanimously" appointed to a new mission station in connection with the Parliamentary Road United Presbyterian Church in Glasgow. The U.P. denomination was formed in 1847 when the United Secession Church and the Relief Church united. On leaving the Scottish Coast Mission his faithful work amongst the sea farers was reflected in an appreciation in the local newspaper which recorded that he had won "not only the respect, but the love of the people in his sphere of labour. His departure from amongst us is much regretted by all, more especially by our fishermen and their families, to whom he has endeared himself by many acts of kindness and attention."[16]

Sadly just six months after leaving St Andrews, Matthew Paterson lost his wife and elder daughter. Both died at home: Sarah died on 22 November 1872[17] followed only three days later by four year old Mary Bella.[18]

Paterson remarried just over a year later on 27 January 1874, this time in Edinburgh to Alison Foggo.[19] Alice, as she was more familiarly known, had been born in East Lothian and was a few years older than her new husband. She died in 1915.[20] Paterson's diary entry concerning his second wife's health – a disease that caused her to be dangerously ill - takes on particular meaning when one realises that it was probably some kind of infectious illness that killed his first wife and daughter.

In 1878 Matthew Paterson was ordained straight from his mission work to take up the responsibilities of Infirmary chaplain taking over from Reverend John H. Topping an English Presbyterian. Paterson served in

---

15 Ruth Allison, Matthew Paterson Research Notes, (2017)
16 *Fife Herald*, (23 May 1872)
17 *Fife Herald*, (28 November 1871)
18 *Greenock Telegraph*, (23 May 1872)
19 Ruth Allison, Matthew Paterson Research Notes, (2017)
20 *The Scotsman*, (5 April 1915)

this post for over 50 years which means he would still have been serving during the inter-war period leading up to the Second World War.[21]

Tragedy was to hit again with the death of his only remaining daughter. The *Greenock Telegraph* announced the death of "Lizzie Graham, the daughter of Rev Matthew Paterson, chaplain of the Royal Infirmary, and the late Sarah Graham" on 20 September 1881.[22] It is interesting to note that Paterson's last diary entry was on the 1 December 1881 and there is no evidence that he continued to keep a diary after this date.

Paterson died in February 1935 being hailed in the Newspaper headlines as "one of the oldest Ministers in Scotland."[23] His body was buried in Sighthill Cemetery in Glasgow.[24]

The diary illustrates a faithful Christian chaplain, from a mission background, working hard for the pastoral and spiritual needs of the patients in a Presbyterian Scotland with authority, integrity and evangelical fervour.

---

21 *The Scotsman* (25 February 1935), p.14
22 *Greenock Telegraph* (30 September 1881), p.2
23 *The Scotsman* (25 February 1935), p.14
24 *The Scotsman* (25 February 1935), p.14

1878

Monday 10th June

Visited 8 wards and read the Scriptures &[25] expounded them in each of the wards. When reading the Scriptures in ward 7 the Night nurse who is a Romanist[26] opened her door & shouted "none of your controversy there and let me sleep I cannot get sleeping for the noise.

Tuesday 11th June

The nurse who interfered with me yesterday was waiting for me this morning to apologise for her conduct yesterday. She said she thought it was The Patients. I accepted her apology & said I would take no notice of it. Visited 8 wards read & expounded the scriptures in 6 of the wards. The nurses agreeable & pleasant

Wednesday 12th June

Read and expounded The Scriptures in all the wards but one, being their receiving day,[27] & Patients were coming in. Both Nurses & Patients very agreeable -

Thursday 13th June

Visited wards 22-21-29-30-28-13-14-221/2. One patient in ward 3- read and expounded the Scriptures in all the wards except one when I prayed – it being near the dinner hour. All the nurses very agreeable-

Monday 17th June

Asked to visit a man in ward 11 who was dying & wished to see me. He is an intelligent man but like many more has lived only for this life. He seems however to realise his awful position & asked me if God would accept him at the eleventh hour. I read several portions & promises of the Scriptures. Ah he said I feel ashamed to come at the last to God after having lived all

---

25 Throughout his diary Paterson uses '&' as well as 'and' I have tried to record his writing accurately so will follow his style throughout.

26 A term commonly used by Protestants for those of the Roman Catholic Faith.

27 This ward would have been Receiving new admissions or perhaps emergency admissions

my life for the world, but I come. I rest on that word "whosoever".[28] I am one of the whosoever & I cast anchor on that. How sad to have wasted one's life and at the last come to God when we can do no better although even then God accepts the Sinner.

Met with a young lad on ward 12 in an anxious state of mind. Also a boy in ward 1 – about 15 years of age earnestly desiring to know the plan of Salvation-

Tuesday 18th June

Called up out of bed to see a young man in ward 20. Visited another in ward 11 whom I had seen during the day. Poor man, he will soon have gone to give in his account & I understand his life has not been a favourable one. The Lord have mercy on his soul.Saw him this afternoon again, but he could not speak. Though he seemed quite conscious& listened to what I said. In visiting the wards (with few exceptions) all are anxious to hear the scriptures read & expounded & in many cases the soil seems prepared & ready to receive the good seed of The Kingdom.

Wednesday 19th June

The man whom I saw in Ward 11 on Monday, died last night. I was told that he had been swearing [at] his wife just a few hours before he died. The character she gave him was a very painful one. Oh how sad to think of a lost soul & I fear he died just as he lived, without God & without hope, though he seemed anxious to be saved from hell. Yet he never seemed to me to have a sense of his lost state and nature-

Thursday 20th June

Visited eight wards and 2 visits to a patient in ward 20 – Had a long conversation with a man upwards of 60 years of age in the Side Room of ward 29- he had been knocked down by a cab[29] on the street and was cut about the head. He said (after I had spoken to him of his state by nature

---

28 Revelation 22:17 King James Version (KJV)
29 This is referring to a horse drawn carriage.

and salvation through faith in Christ), "I have been lying here for three weeks & my whole life has been brought up before me. Sometimes I have lived well enough at other times I have been very foolish. My wife had 15 children[30] to me" one was killed, 6 were dead and 8 were still alive & all married, but [for] two who lived with him till he met with this accident – Since he had come into The Infirmary his furniture had been sold to pay the rent, & when he went out he did not know where to go & he wept like a child. I tried to comfort him by directing him to The Friend of the Lonely and Saviour of Sinners. I read several portions of The Scriptures, showing that Jesus was able to save; I then prayed, when over he was still bathed in tears, & thanked me for my interest in him. I promised to look back soon again-

Friday 21st June

I saw a man this forenoon in ward 27- who had been brought in the previous day, his lorry[31] having gone over him. I went in the afternoon to see him again & his body had just been carried to the dead house. Lord help me to be in earnest about the people's souls in this house – every day some poor Soul and sometimes more take their journey into the eternal world to tender their account to God, & I fear a great many of them are not prepared. Too often they die as they have lived.

Monday 24th June

Nothing of particular notice in visiting. The people anxious to hear the Scriptures read and to be prayed with. Even the Catholics listen most attentively while I am addressing those beside them ~

Tuesday 25th June

Met with a young lad in ward 12- whom I saw last week in a very anxious state of mind. He seems today more calm & said he was not so burdened as when I saw him last. I asked what he thought had made him better,

---

30 It would appear that 2 out of his 15 children still stayed at home. His loss was far reaching

31 Prior to 1911 the word *Lorry* tended to refer to a large horse-drawn goods wagon

because he was trusting now in Jesus as his Sav.[32] (*sic*) & had found peace. He said he was anxious to get better. Still if he did not, he had [not] the fear of death that he had last week when I saw him. He seemed so bright & happy –

Wednesday 26th June

Saw a painful case today when I was visiting ward 22- A woman brought in who had cut her throat. I saw the wound & certainly it was not a pleasant sight. When looking at her I thought that the only thing that made me differ from her was the grace of God. But for grace where would I have been –

Monday 1st July

Visited wards 1-3-4-14-9-10-11. Nothing particular today in visitation. It is very pleasant to observe how anxious people are to listen to the words of eternal life.

Oh My God help me to be faithful in dealing with the people about their souls. Give me the Spirit of prayer & fill me with the Holy Ghost for Jesus sake-

Tuesday 2nd July

Visited a boy in ward 15 whose parents are members of Plantation U.P.Ch.[33] While speaking to him regarding his great Sal. he told me he had given his heart to Jesus last Sabbath Day. Saw a most humbling sight of an old man of about 70 years of age who had destroyed himself with drink and women, his whole body was ulcerated through his bad life.[34] How true 'that the way of transgressors is hard.'[35]

---

32 2 Paterson uses the abbreviation Sal. for Salvation through faith in Christ Jesus as the atoning sacrifice for sin.
33 United Presbyterian Church
34 This could have been the result of a sexually transmitted disease as well as alcohol abuse.
35 Reference to Proverbs 13:15 KJV

Wednesday 3rd July

Saw a young man today who got his arm taken off by the elbow. It began, he told me from a scratch on the finger.[36] A very little thing and yet to save his life, he had to lose his arm. Little sins seem little things, but we must either part with them or lose our Soul –another young man was told when he first came into the Infirmary that his leg would have to be amputated in order that his life might be saved. He would not consent for a long time. At last he consented when it was too late & he died.

Thursday 4th July

Speaking to the nurse inward 3- She told me that the man[37] who addressed the patients on Sundays was in the habit of using language that often excited[38] the patients. This is the same person who told the boy that he would be dead before another Sabbath and would be lost if he did not believe. The boy when I saw him was in a very excited state, but became calm after I stated to him the plan of Redemption –

Friday 5th July

The nurse in ward 24 – had the same complaint as the nurse in ward 3 – that often the patients had been very much excited after being visited by certain parties & was frequently much the worse of it –

Tuesday 9th July

In ward 4 I found 3 patients very ill & in speaking to one of them a young lad he told me his trouble was so great that he could not think on anything else but his trouble. Another illustration of the danger in putting off Sal. To a deathbed. The Lord help me to be faithful in dealing with souls.

---

36 Probably Sepsis or Gangrene
37 Identity unknown, possibly a member from one of the local churches.
38 'Excited' was often used as a term to describe distress.

Wednesday 10th July

A very solemn scene in ward 27. Was sent for to pray with a young lad who had met with an accident at the Glas. & S.W. St.[39] I went but found that he was too far gone to be able to enter into a conversation with me. I prayed however believing that God hears & we are commanded to pray & let our requests be made known unto God; after which he shortly departed this life without ever realising his awful position. I saw him after he departed this life his body was fearfully mangled. Such a sight I shall not soon forget. Oh how humbling. I tried to improve the circumstance with the other patients & to press on them the necessity of being ready to meet their God. Speaking to a man in ward 4 who is every day becoming weaker, I said I hope you are resting on Jesus & looking to Him as all your Sal. "I do not hope" he replied but I am sure that I am. How seldom do we hear a testimony like this "I am sure that I am" It is oftener "I hope that I am trusting in Jesus to save me"-

Thursday 11th July

Nothing of any importance, at least nothing but what one sees every day. Sickness, and death. Spoke to a man in ward 4 in the forenoon. Went back to see him in the afternoon but he had departed this life. Twice I have taken tracts from the side room into the ward 29 which have been removed by some party or parties −[40]

Monday 15th July

I met with a most interesting case in ward 3 who told me that he had given his heart to the Lord Jesus since he had come into the house. I asked when he had found peace. He could not exactly say but the truth had just been gradually dawning upon him & last night the word preached in the Chapel had been very precious to him.

---

39 Glasgow and South Western Railway was formed on 28th October 1850 running from Bridge St Glasgow to Ayr. It grew with several acquisitions and in1878 opened the Largs Branch.www.railwaysarchives.co.uk has some 900 pages of Railway accidents dating back to early 1800s.
40 See Monday 10th June entry. .

Tuesday 16th July

Saw a young man in Ward 3 who is very weak & evidently dying. He expressed his trust in the Lord Jesus as all his salvation & all his desire. Met with a woman in ward 10 who professed to find peace by believing in the Lord Jesus while speaking to her. Saw another from Busby[41] who realizes Christ to be very precious to her soul ~

Wednesday 17th July

I was requested to visit a man who was dying in Ward 25- & a poor woman in ward 22 – also desired to see me both so weak that they could not enter into conversation, I endeavoured to set plainly before them the simple plan of Redemption[42] through the Mediator[43] Jesus Christ. But oh it is difficult to speak to one who has put off till then their peace with God- however one feels it to be their duty to hold up Christ before their eyes to the very last moment –

Thursday 18th July

Visited Ward 3 to see a man who I believed was dying when I last saw him & I found that he had departed this life. Met with a patient in Ward 1whose case seems to be rather interesting. I spoke to him& what seemed to be his difficulty was that he could not see how God could forgive the sinner all at once. I endeavoured to show him that justification was an act. The thing of a moment. but that same –was a work- Was very much cheered in conversation with several of the patients ~

Friday 19th July

The patient whom I saw in Ward 1 yesterday is in a more hopeful state today. He is trusting in Christ but thought he could not be right as he

---

41 Busby was a small manufacturing town about 5 miles south of Glasgow.
42 Rev Paterson probably referring to Acts 4 where the Apostle Peter addresses the Sanhedrin explaining that Redemption or Salvation is through one Mediator between man and God
43 The Mediator is Jesus Christ.

had wandering thoughts.[44] After some conversation with him & showing that we needed to be continually trusting and coming to the blood[45] for cleansing he appeared to understand it more fully & see it clearer than he had ever done. I never he said, "Saw it in that light before". He was truly thankful to me for explaining to him the way of salvation~

It really cheers & refreshes one's Soul to see how readily the People generally enter into conversation concerning the things that belong to their peace –

Saturday 20th July

I was asked to visit a woman in Ward 10 at her own request. Yesterday the Priest[46] had given her absolution[47] and from the moment he left she felt that she was a Sinner& became very anxious about her soul. The nurse told me that the trouble about her soul last night was worse than her trouble of body. I asked if she wished me to have conversation with her, 'Yes' she replied & she narrated to me her whole history & what had passed between the Priest & her. I then read to her several promises from the New Test[48] bearing on the plan of Salvation & how we become reconciled to God and prayed with her. At first she thought God would not forgive her as she had been a great sinner. I asked if she thought God would forgive some of her sins, Oh Yes. She thought perhaps little sins but not her great sins. I read, 'The blood of Jesus Christ cleanseth from all sin' and showed that when God pardoned one sin all were pardoned. I dwelt for a little and repeated it, 'all sin'. Oh she said, I see it, I see it and all that I have got to do is just believe.

---

44 For the Christian, the act of sanctification is one of being made Holy, set apart, 'cleansed. 'Sanctification is an ongoing process throughout life..

45 Hebrew 9:22 'coming to the blood' probably refers to the atoning sacrifice of Jesus Christ.

46 This refers to the Roman Catholic cleric

47 For Paterson 'absolution' or 'pardon for sin' can only be granted by God. The pardon for all followed the sacrificial death of Jesus Christ. Therefore no human can absolve the guilt of mankind. See also 38. For the Roman Catholic Church 'absolution' is considered a sacrament which prepares the soul for death through penance, sacramental grace, prayers and anointing..

48 New Testament

Monday 22nd July

Visited the Roman Catholic woman yesterday before service & today again. She seems to be in a most hopeful state of mind & has professed to find peace by believing in The Lord Jesus Christ-

Tuesday 23rd July

In ward one the patient I speak of in page 13, whom I saw first in an anxious state, then in a hopeful state, is now I have no doubt resting on the Lord Jesus –He expressed to me today his firm belief in Christ as his Saviour. I cannot say in all the wards visited today, that I saw much anxiety (if any at all) after Spiritual things. One man in Ward 15, only new in, I suppose he had not seen the Doctor, rather opposed what I had been saying to the others, by speaking of the future as a dark road & speaking of the Bible as being a doubtful record of God's mind & will. He spoke of not understanding this part and that other part. I asked if he understood himself. He replied, 'No man did that', why then I said Can you understand God who inhabiteth eternity-

Wednesday 24th July

The Roman Catholic in Ward 10 seems to me a most hopeful case of conversion. Two interesting cases in Ward 18 – both seem to be anxiously inquiring. The one is a married woman from Govan, an amputation of the foot. The other a girl from Slamanan[49] [*sic*]-

Thursday 25th July

I was asked to see a young lad in W.12 – about 17 years of age. I first saw him about the middle of last month when he was in a very anxious state of mind, then I saw him again on the 25th when he told me that he felt calm and peaceful. I asked him what he thought had given him the peace of mind which he now had. He replied because I am now trusting in the Sav.[50] & have found peace. I have seen him every week since & so far as I

---

49 Slamannan is a small village 4.6 miles (7.4 km) south-west of Falkirk.
50 Abbreviation for Saviour.

could judge he was now resting upon in Christ for his salvation. Saw him twice today. He said that if it was the Lord's will he was resting alon (*sic*) [alone] in Christ for his salvation. He said that if it was The Lord's will he was quite prepared to go. That Christ was all his Salvation & all his desire. After I had spoken and prayed with him he asked another patient to help him up a little in the [bed], then taking him by the hand he said, 'Jamie will you meet me in Heaven.' It was too much for the old man, he could not answer the question, & I observed him wiping a tear from his eye, while the young lad continued to speak to him concerning his everlasting salvation. He bade me farewell & said, 'I will meet you in Heaven.'

Friday 26th July

Visited the Roman Catholic woman in W.10. She told me she had had a visit of the Priest today & told him that she had renounced their Creed, as she could find no comfort or peace in it. The first question he asked was had the Chaplain been speaking to her?[51] Her reply was that it was at her request. I thank God that she has been enabled to make a good confession. She told me that she was happier in her own soul since she had told him that she wished to have no more to do with him.

The young lad, David Cooper, who requested to see me yesterday, died last night about ½ past 7 o'clock

Tuesday 30th July

Had an interesting conversation with nurse in Ward 10. I have spoken to her several times. Today she asked a tract from me, which was a good opportunity to speak to her. She told me she had a desire to know the Saviour but could not understand the way. I endeavoured to make it as plain as possible by several illustrations & told her just to trust the Saviour & take Him at his word –

---

51 Another example of the suspicion between Roman Catholic and Protestant clerics in Paterson's era.

Wednesday 31st July

Had interesting conversations with several of the patients. Others again seem to be hardened & indifferent as if they had no Soul to be saved.

Tuesday 6th August

Though I have taken no note of what has transpired in the wards since last Wed. yet I have to praise my God for the opportunity in commending the Saviour to the sick and dying. I have just left the bedside of a poor man whom I do not expect to see again. He had been knocked down a stair & by the fall his back was broken. He seems to suffer very much pain & is evidently sinking. I prayed with him & commended him to The God of all grace who is able & willing to save all who come to him by Jesus Christ.

Wednesday 7th August

I saw an interesting case today illustrating the plan of Salvation which I endeavoured to point and apply to several of the patients.

A young man had gone through an operation this morning & as I understand they could not stop the bleeding & the poor fellow was sinking in their hands. They cut the arm of another patient & let his blood flow into the veins of the dying man,& so saved his life.[52] 'The blood is the life there of'.[53] It was the blood of another that Saved the dying man. It is the blood of Christ that saves the dying sinner. Nothing but the blood.

Thursday 8th August

Visited the Roman Catholic woman in W. 10. She is very weak & from her appearance it is evident that her days are very few. She had very little to say, indeed she was not able to speak much.

Saw the man whose back is broken in W.25 he is very weak & suffers a good deal of pain. He expressed his confidence & trust in the finished

---

52 Probably an early example of blood transfusion
53 Paterson was aware of many dying through loss of blood and recognised an analogy between blood transfusion saving the patient and Christ's blood saving a lost humankind.

work of Jesus. I sometimes do not know what to think of people who all their life have lived regardless of God & Salvation, yet when they come to die without ever any sign of Repentance, or sorrow for their past life, with confidence, not even a shadow of doubt, express their trust in the Lord Jesus as their Saviour. I hope it is real but I cannot help sometimes thinking it must be a delusion-

Friday 9th August

The man whom I saw yesterday in W.25 died today just a few minutes before I entered the ward. Sent for to see the Roman Catholic in W.10 who wished to see me before she departed this life. Read & prayed with her –

Monday 12th August

Nothing of any particular interest today. Some very glad to see me, others quite indifferent. Though some of them it is quite evident will never be better yet no anxiety about their soul or salvation through Christ-

Friday 30th August

Began duty today after a fortnight holiday, feeling very much the better of it. While visiting Ward 12 I observed a man who was very low & evidently in a dying state. Looking at the card I saw that he was a (R.C.) & I therefore passed on. I halted & spoke to the Nurse & looking round I observed him waving with his hand. I went back, he told me he was a R.C. but he wished me to read to him. I very gladly responded to his request. I read a portion of a tract on the death & sufferings of our Lord & several portions of Scripture which I expounded. All bearing on the death of Christ, man's state by nature & the necessity of regeneration by the Holy Spirit, after which I prayed. The poor man was most attentive and hoped that I would come soon again & see him -

Tuesday 3rd September

Visited 6 wards had personal conversation with a number of the Patients who conversed freely with me on the things pertaining to their eternal peace – prayed in several of the wards.

Wednesday 4th September

All the patients very attentive & I observed several in tears after I had read & spoken with them. Very few indeed who object to conversation on eternal things though there are exceptional cases. Suffering in their case seems only to harden them & to make them more determined to fight against God -

Thursday 5th September

When I returned from dinner today a cab was standing at the door which leads into the Surgical Wards & several of the convalescent patients were standing around the cab, which led me to inquire if it was a serious case & the reply I got was, they thought he was badly hurt from the moans they heard. I entered Ward 16 & saw the poor man lying on a bed with the doctor & nurse trying to soothe him. I began to talk to him on the necessity of composing himself & looking away from all that was human to the Saviour of Sinners. But the poor man was suffering so much that I saw it was impossible he could listen. I engaged in prayer commending him to The God of all grace to have mercy upon his soul & in a few minutes after, he breathed his last. Even in his last moments his cry was lift me up or give me a drink 'turn me' he would say or 'lift me' up. Then I will listen to you'. How many in health act this way put off their great Salvation from time to time untill (*sic*) it is too late. I was pleased with the nurse who spoke to him & tried to direct his mind to the Lord Jesus Christ, but he seemed to take (no)[54] notice of what she said –

Friday 6th September

Visited Ward 1-2-3-4-5-6-12 read & prayed in those where I saw it convenient. Read & prayed with the R.C. in ward 12- He was so weak as

54 Typographical error in original text 'to' instead of 'no'.

to be unable to speak to me but was quite conscious & understood what I was saying. Also read & prayed aloud in the ward so that all might hear.

Monday 9th September

While visiting Ward 23 I was about to speak to a woman who had gone through an operation on Friday. The nurse came forward and said O Mr Paterson I can't allow you to speak to that patient. Then she added you know it is by the Doctor's orders. I made no reply but read & prayed aloud so that all the patients in the ward heard me-[55]

Wednesday 11th September

Read and prayed in several of the wards. The patients upon the whole attentive & interested if one might judge from outward appearance. Visited an old man in W 2 who is dying. I repeated several passages of Scripture, describing our lost state by nature, & salvation through faith in The Lord Jesus, but he seemed too far gone to comprehend what I said & was not inclined to enter into conversation with me: though he requested me to pray for him, That The Lord would have mercy on his soul. I engaged in prayer & when I had finished he seemed to be quite unconscious I spoke to him again & asked if he had any friends, but he seemed unwilling to give me any information on this point –

Thursday 12th September

Visited 6 wards and made one visit to ward 27-

Friday 13th September

As I entered ward 7 this afternoon my attention was drawn to a young man who from his anxious look led me to think he wished conversation with me. It would be needless to enter into the details of his whole history, but though he was only 21 years of age his career had been a very sad one. When a boy he had been sent to a Boarding School & with plenty of money in his

---

55 By reading from the Bible and praying aloud Paterson would have been hoping that the patient would hear and respond quietly where he lay.

back pocket & companions likeminded with himself he had taken to drink which leads to every other sin.[56] At last he had left this country & had gone to Canada & began to work as a labourer at a railway bridge but gradually his strength began to fail & when he consulted a doctor he was told his lungs were affected & to go home at once. It was while he was working as a labourer that he had been led to think on his sin and folly. A minister of the Gospel[57] there had taken a deep interest in him & had kindly spoken to him regarding his Soul's Salvation & last June he had been enabled to rest on Jesus for Salvation. "I have however" he said received great blessing from the tract you gave me the last time you were here. Title 'What is believing'[?].[58] I have never read anything that has done me so much good", & holding up the tract in his hand he said, with a smile I will not part with this tract." An old man lying in the bed next (to) him asked me if I had another of the same as it had been read by all the ward.

Monday 16th September

Visited several very bad cases in ward 5 – One of them a young man from my old district who occasionally attended my meetings in Dobbie's Loan.[59] I have the satisfaction in knowing that he is prepared for the Great Change, having accepted Christ about 2 years ago – Died the same evening about 6 o'clock -

Friday 20th September

I saw a very bad case brought into ward 3 of poisoning through drink. I understand the man had been drinking heavily. All such cases are generally the effects of strong drink – while reading the Scriptures in ward 6 the Priest came marching in thinking I suppose that I would stop but I went on reading & when he saw this he at once retracted his steps & went down

---

56 Alcohol abuse was rife and led to the birth of the Temperance movement. This abuse was probably blamed for Societal decline in Paterson's day.

57 Paterson is probably referring to an evangelical minister.

58 This may have been a tract from the Tractarian society or Oxford movement.

59 Dobbies Loan is a road in Glasgow that is still in existence and possibly dates back to an original Roman Road.

stairs. I have no doubt feeling that he did not always get things all his own way.

Monday 23rd September

Speaking to a patient in ward 24 – who came in on Saturday. After listening to him [on] how he met with the accident I directed him to The Great Physician, The Lord Jesus, "Ah yes" he said "I know him, He is no stranger to me." & gave me his history [of] how he had been brought to the Lord Jesus, about 10 months ago. The big man wept like a child as we talked about the love of Christ

Tuesday 24th September

Nothing particular in my visitation today. The Surgical wards are being painted & the patients are being removed to one ward after another, so that it is sometimes difficult to get anything like a conversation with them as there is always such a walking hither and thither in the wards ~

Wednesday 25th September

Saw a young lad in Ward 9 – who has been in the house for sometime. He appears now from what he said today to be thinking on those things which belong to his eternal peace. I had a pleasant conversation with him & I trust also profitable –

Thursday 26th September

Met with an interesting case of a young lad in Ward 3. He told me he had been thinking seriously about his Soul for sometime & had tried hard but always failed: like many more I found he was trying to work out a righteousness of his own. I asked him if he thought he was a Sinner. No he replied, I have never done anything bad. But I said have you ever told a lie! Yes. Did you ever swear! Not very often. But you have sworn? Yes, when angry. Well I said, you have committed one sin& that is you have not loved the Lord with all your heart. No. Well you are under the broken law & therefore under the curse, and being under the curse you are under condemnation. I then endeavoured to point out to him how The Lord Jesus had taken our place & perfectly obeyed The Law & suffered in our room & stead[60], & by believing in Him we have eternal life. The young man whom I notice in page 27 told me today that there was no hope of him getting better, but he was happy in The Lord, so full of the Love of Christ that he had been constrained to call some of the patients to his bedside & tell them of the love and joy he had experienced in having trusted Christ as his Saviour. 'I [could] not, he said, help telling them what The Lord had done (to) my Soul-

Thursday 3rd October

I was about to engage in prayer in Ward 6 and announced my intention to do so, when a Roman Catholic woman said, 'Pray awa' Yes but I said put down your paper while I pray. She did it, though not very willing – In Ward 11 I was about to do the same, when a man declined to shut his book. I told him to put down his book while I read & prayed, after I was finished & had seen the patients I told him to read the Rules[61] & to remember that he must submit to them –I also spoke to the woman in Ward 6 & told her that if she did the same again I would report her to the Superintendent.[62] She seemed rather taken aback. –

Tuesday 8th October

The work among the patients goes on quietly. It is cheering as well as encouraging to notice how eagerly they receive tracts & how attentive when spoken to regarding the Salvation of their precious Soul -

Friday 11th October

Nothing of special interest. The people upon the whole always glad to see me. One Patient in Ward 16 who met with his accident through drink seems interested in what I say to him & professes to be very penitent.

---

60 'room and stead' - in our place.
61 Rules for Royal Infirmary patient's can be found in a publication collated by one Henry Lammond Secretary Glasgow Royal Infirmary http://www.archives.gla.ac.uk/gghb/
62 This probably refers to the Superintendent Nurse a senior hospital figure akin to a Matron.

Tuesday 15th October

I desire to record my thanks and praise to God for his mercies to me in having spared my wife to me who was seized with inflammation on Saturday morning, and was dangerously ill for about 24 hours being about that time before the disease was checked. She is still very weak but I trust that with great care and with good nursing she may soon recover again. May The Lord comfort and strengthen her is my earnest prayer –

Visited four wards today but did not feel so much in the Spirit as I would desire. Lord quicken me for Thy Name Sake Amen –

Wednesday 16th October

I have to thank my God for blessing vouchsafed to be soul today. I was much helped in speaking to the patients, had more liberty & was enabled to deal faithfully with the people regarding their great Salvation –

Wednesday October 23rd

While I have had during the last eight days much profitable & pleasant conversations with the patients throughout the wards yet, I have had nothing of very special interest. One told me today that he enjoyed worship in the chapel in the evening & wished that I would be as long (along) again-

Friday 25th October

I have just now come from the bedside of an old man newly come into ward 16 – from Kilsyth. He is very seriously hurt. I spoke and prayed with him. He evidently is well acquainted with scriptures. When I repeated a promise he at once catched (*sic*) it up & repeated it after me.

Monday 28th October

I had a pleasant conversation with a patient in ward 21 (A farmer from Dunkeld) he told me he had often thought of the necessity in having peace made up with God but somehow always put it off from the fact he supposed that he could not understand how peace was to be found. I endeavoured to put clearly before his mind the plan of salvation. He said it was clear but he supposed that it was its simplicity that made it the stumbling block –

A young man in the same ward (a Roman Catholic) expressed a desire to learn to read & I promised to get him a spelling book –

Tuesday 29th October

The most interesting case I met with in my rounds was an old man in ward 16. He seems a warm hearted old Christian & full of the Spirit of Prayer. My soul was refreshed from what he told me of his experience in The Lord's dealings with him –

Thursday 31st October

When reading and praying in ward 7 today I observed 3 patients who appeared specially interested in what I had read and expounded. One of them a car washer[63] I found afterwards to be in an anxious state of mind. Indeed nothing encourages me so much in the work as to see how anxious the Patients upon the whole are to hear The Scriptures read –

Wednesday 6th November

Visited ward 7 today and found that the car washer had died the following day after I saw him. What a lesson it is for me to deal honestly & faithfully with the patients regarding their immortal souls.

Monday 11th November

Was asked to see a young man last night in ward 5. Spoke & prayed with him he died this morning. I should mention that I saw him on Friday last & when speaking to him about his great Salvation he said it was too often put off to the last. Nothing of any particular interest in the wards today. The patients generally willing enough to enter into religious conversation (with the exception of the Romanist) who looks at me sometimes as if I had

---

63 Carriage Washer

no right to be there. I am certain from what I see that if they had the power we protestants would not have an inch of liberty.[64]

Friday15th November

The nurse of ward 11 told me of the happy death of a little boy whom I spoke and prayed with last time I was in the ward. He died the day after I saw him. A short time before he departed this life he clasped his little hands together & looking up to heaven prayed "Lord Jesus come into my life & take me this evening to Thyself" –

Saw another in ward 11 today who is dying but is safe in the arms of Jesus. He told me when he was led to the knowledge of the Truth –another in the same ward in an enquiring state of mind -

Monday 18th November

Nothing very special tho I was cheered and encouraged with the free and open manner in which a number of the patients entered into conversation with me, concerning their soul's salvation. Oh for the power of the Holy Ghost in my own soul. Lord Baptise me with fire & with the Holy Ghost so that I may deal with souls as one who must give an account to God for my stewardship –

Wednesday 20th November

Met with 2 interesting cases in ward 20 – both in an enquiring state of mind, one of them a native of Fife (Cellardyke)

Thursday 21st November

Though I have met nothing of real inquiry, yet, upon the whole the people seem anxious to be spoken to regarding their great Sal. & I have no difficulty in getting them to enter freely into conversation with me on Spiritual Subjects

64 See footnote 29

Friday 22nd November

Visited 8 wards in the Medical side today. Several of the patients it was evident were in the last Stage of Consumption.[65] How solemnizing it is to feel that one is speaking for the last time to one, who will soon appear before God. The Lord keep me to be faithful in dealing with immortal souls.

Monday 25th November

I had much liberty in speaking to the patients today, & I thank God for grace given so that I was enabled in some measure to deal faithfully with the people of their sin & danger & their need of Sal. through faith in Christ.

Tuesday 26th November

Saw my two friends in ward 20 who are still tossing on the sea of doubts and fears. Had a long conversation with them & prayed but all seemed dark to them. How vain is the help of man in the matter of a Sinner's Salvation. I think if there is a moment in one's life that we feel our weakness, it is when speaking to an anxious soul -

Wednesday 27th November

Visited (McLerie)[66] in Ward 5 whom I was asked to visit last night after worship. He is very weak so that I could not enter into conversation with him regarding his Salvation. How sad that the one thing needful should be put off till a deathbed, as it is the case with thousands & many are the regrets I hear from the lips of the dying.

Monday 2nd December

While on my way home last night from the Infirmary at the close of my service, after having passed the receiving gate, something led me to turn & ask Andrew (the gateman)[67] if any serious cases had been admitted since

---

65 Tuberculosis
66 Name unclear
67 Probably refers to a Gate keeper

Saturday, when he told me of a woman in Ward 26 who had cut her throat. It so happened that she had been anxious, or at least expressed a desire to see me. I spoke & prayed with her. The poor creature seemed very penitent & while I continued to direct her to the Lord Jesus as Saviour of Sinners. She listened most attentively & appeared to find some comfort from these words. The blood of Jesus Christ cleanseth us from all sin. I saw her today again but Mrs McPherson had just left her& she seemed exhausted & had fallen into a quiet sleep. I did not trouble her. May the Lord have mercy on her Soul.

Tuesday 3rd December

I was asked when I had just come in this morning to see a young girl in ward 7 who was dying. She was just about 19 years of age. I spoke to her of the Love of Jesus in dying on the cross for our sins when she replied that she had her peace made up with God. I questioned her as to the foundation of her hope & was delighted to find that she was trusting alone in the Lord Jesus for her salvation –

Friday 6th December

I had a most interesting conversation with a young woman (who belongs to Hamilton) in ward 6. She is in an enquiring sate of mind I must see her soon again.

Monday 9th December

Had a fair attendance at the Service last night in the Chapel, about 40 present. I have observed the young woman that I had conversation with in Ward 6, attending regularly the Chapel every night. Made two visits at the close of the service. Wards 22-29. I have seen today a most interesting little fellow in W. 17. He has gone through an operation of amputation of the foot. He told me his father ran away & left his mother & his mother went to look for his father & never came back. I quoted 'when my father and mother forsake me then the Lord will take me up.'[68] But before I had got to the end he repeated the verse& seemed to know it well. I asked him if

68 Psalm 27:10

the Lord had taken him up. Oh yes he said Jesus has raised up kind friends to look after me. He then told me that he was at an industrial school,[69] and repeated to me the prayer which he said night & morning to God his heavenly Father.

Wednesday 11th December

Visited 8 wards today & thank my God that I have been enabled through grace to tell the poor and suffering of the true Friend. The Saviour of Sinners. O my God who is sufficient for the work? I frequently tremble when I am passing through the wards & see so many sick & suffering & the majority on the wrong side, without God and without hope. Help me to be faithful in speaking to people regarding their great salvation.

Friday 13th December

Saw the little boy in ward 17 who loves The Lord Jesus. He is in Mossbank industrial school & told me that the Governor had worship every night. In our conversation, he said, he loved the Sav. & would not give him up for The World.

Monday 16th December

No very special case today in the wards I visited. The patients appear to be always glad to see me, & ready to enter into conversation on Religious Subjects

Visited a patient in Ward 6 in the Side Room who requested to see me. I found her in a very anxious state of mind. She appeared a little more calm after I had conversed with he r& in simple language explained the plan of Salvation. I was pleased to see a patient in the ward reading to another, & was all the more delighted when she told me that she was converted 6 years ago.

---

69 A school for educating neglected children or delinquents

Friday 20th December

Nearly another week ended and in looking back over the week's labours I am led to ask myself the question what have I done? Has there been any good accomplished in my visitations to the sick and dying? I often feel sad at the indifference manifested when I am speaking to the people. In some cases there seems a ray of light, and a desire on their part to listen to the story of the cross. In others there is no ground to work upon. Ignorance and great darkness, and no desire for light.

Tuesday 24th December

I was speaking to the little boy in ward 17 – that I have referred to already in page 41[70]- I said to him "Do you think Jesus would save you if you were to die?" "Yes" was his reply. But I said, How do you think Jesus will save a little boy like you? What foundation have you to suppose that you would be saved?' The little boy looked me straight in the face and said, Because Jesus says "Him that cometh to me I will in no wise cast out."[71]

His name is William Queen and is 11 years of age.

Monday 30th December

Though I noted nothing down since last week it is not that I have had no very interesting conversations because scarcely a day passes, but I meet with some case of interest. Some patient needing to be comforted, another anxiously inquiring and has to be pointed to Christ, The Saviour, or one who once knew the Lord & has backslidden.[72]& has to be told of Christ's willingness to receive them back into the fold again.

70 Mon. 9th Dec.
71 John 6:37 KJV
72 Hosea 14:4

1879

Thursday 2nd January

Another year 1878 past away as [if] it had never been and yet when one calls up the past year with all its changes there are periods, which can never be forgotten. It has been to many a year of the deepest sorrow, The failure of the City of Glasgow Bank.[73] It has been the quietest New Year I have spent for many years, and yet one of the happiest as it was truly to me a holiday (in the real sense of the word) which I have not enjoyed on New Year's day for a long time. At the annual meeting[74] of Nurses in the Infirmary, after which I went through a number of wards with my wife – I have at the same time to record my thanks with the deepest gratitude to My God for blessings temporal & spiritual during the past year. He has truly led me in ways that I knew not off [sic] (& never expected) In giving me the glorious field to labour in for the conversion of precious souls. Lord do Thou help me to [be] faithful in this part of thy Vineyard. Oh that I may pray more earnestly for The Salvation of precious Souls.

Wednesday 8th January

A week of the New year already past & what have I done? I am always forming new resolutions to be more faithful & more earnest about the Sal. of precious Souls and these resolutions are too often I fear no sooner made than broken. Lord give me grace, more grace, that I may be more prayerful, more watchful for souls, as one that must give account.

Friday 10th January

I saw a sad case today in Ward 11 a young man dying & he said he did not know if he would be Saved, he did not think it, as he had put off till now & he believed it was too late now. I endeavoured to show him that though he had put off till now, yet Christ was able and willing to save him if he as a sinner accepted Christ as his Saviour. With all I said [I] could not persuade

---

73 For more information see article on Bank Of England's website. Desperate adventurers and men of straw: the failure of City of Glasgow Bank and its enduring impact on the UK banking system by Richard Button and Samuel Knott of the Bank's Financial Stability Strategy and Risk Directorate, and Conor Macmanus and Matthew Willison of the Bank's Prudential Policy Directorate.

74 As per Constitution of Glasgow Royal Infirmary see footnote 53

him to believe he would be Saved. Though I argued & quoted promise after promise.

Monday 13th January

I was asked to visit a patient dying in Ward 9, like the majority I found he was seeking Sal. at the eleventh hour when he could do no better, anxious to be saved from everlasting punishment. I often feel sad to think that men should all their lives serve the devil,[75] and at the end of an ill spent life seek Sal. when they can do no better. I felt it however to be my duty to set before him The Way of Life, and the ability of Christ to save all who come to him.

Tuesday 14th January

I saw a woman yesterday in Ward 23 – very low and evidently dying. She told me when she first came in that she was a backslider[76] and was in a very anxious state of mind regarding her Soul's Salvation. I encouraged herby the special promises given to the backslider in God's word to return & she would be received. I have reason to hope she was restored to the Divine favour, though she never enjoyed a sense of The Lord's forgiveness. Today I was on my way to see her when I heard she had died this morning.

Wednesday 15th January

I saw a patient yesterday in ward 20 spoke and prayed with him. Called today to see him. The bed was empty, which told me he had gone to tender his account to God. I often feel awfully solemnized when speaking to the people here as I am often dealing with them and urging them for the last time to accept of God's great Sal. through Jesus Christ.

Thursday 16th January

I spoke to a patient in ward 11 in the side room who is very low & no hope of recovery. I began to talk to him regarding his future hope when he

---

75 Matthew 6:24 No man can serve two masters. Paterson is suggesting that rejecting Christ is synonymous with accepting the devil.
76 Somebody who came to faith but has since drifted

begged of me not to trouble him as he was so weak. I said I did not wish to trouble him but it was of great importance that he should get his peace made up with God as he was evidently dying. I proposed we should join in prayer. Again he wished me if I prayed not to be long. It was very different from another in the same ward who entered freely into conversation with me & was anxious to secure his great salvation~

Friday 17th January

I have had several very interesting conversations today with the patients, and one which I think deserves to be specially noticed. A young man in Ward 5 whom I have again & again been speaking to as I saw he was dying. He was however quite indifferent and often appeared as if he would be glad to get rid of me. Thou [Though] I still kept going to him and pleading with him to be reconciled to God. Today he expressed a wish for conversation, and a desire to get his peace made up with God. I sat down beside him and we had a long chat together; and from the anxious look he sometimes gave me it was evident that he was receiving and appreciating what I said.- The Lord give him light and peace –

Tuesday 21st January

Visited a case last night and twice today in Ward 25 who met with an accident yesterday morning at Cowlairs Station[77] and has lost both his arms below the elbow, and one foot. He seems favourable and requested me toread a few verses to him, which I did and afterwards prayed. So far as I could judge and from what he has said indeed from the very manner in which he has expressed himself to me, he seems to be trusting in the finished work of Christ.

Wednesday 22nd January

Dr Marshall Lang[78] and Mr Wilson of Crammond held a service in the Chapel this afternoon, which was well attended and the addresses were of

---

77 Cowlairs Station was a railway station on the Glasgow to Edinburgh line. It opened 21st February 1842 and closed to passengers on 7th September 1964
78 This could be a reference to Rev Dr John Marshall Lang www.theglasgowstory.com

a most impressive nature, calculated to do great good. The Lord own the word in the conversion of precious Souls.

Thursday 23rd January

Had a most interesting conversation with a patient in Ward 11 who was at one time most unwilling to be spoken to about his Soul. He seems now to [be] the opposite, most anxious to enter into conversation on Spiritual Things.

Friday 24th January

The young man that I took a note of in Ward 5 on the 17th who appeared a little more hopeful from his conversation was today as careless and indifferent about his Soul as he has ever been; thou[gh] dying he will not believe it, and thinks he will get better. I pleaded hard with him to get his peace made up with God and then he would have two strings to his bow, whether living or dying he would be The Lord's. I asked him if he read the last tract I gave him. Yes, he said, but just in the same way I would read newspapers; it has no other effect, I had just to leave him, in the way I found him, unmoved. But before I left I warned him faithfully of his state before God and the eternity that was before him if he died unsaved. I told him that his blood would be upon his own head, as I had come to him again and again with the message of God's love in Christ, also the freeness of Sal. had been set before him.

My own experience is this, that this young man is but an illustration of the majority of those who have up to a deathbed lived without God, and without hope. They too often die as they have lived hardened in Sin and "past feeling".

Thursday 30th January

When I entered ward 6 this morning I saw the priest giving the Sacrament to a poor creature who was dying. I of course took no notice of him, but attended my own duties. A little after Mrs McPhearson came in while I was in the side room. It seemed she had been speaking to this woman yesterday and she had requested her to call again today again for conversation. When the priest saw Mrs McPhearson go up and speak to the woman He said, "Don't speak to that woman she is a Roman Catholic." This had taken place when I was in the side room. She came to me and asked what she would do. I said "If the woman wish[es] you to have conversation with her do it. By all means speak to her. I prayed in the ward and left Mrs McPhearson, with the view of commending Christ and His Sal. to the poor woman~

Monday 3rd February

I was asked last night at the close of the service to visit a patient in Ward 5 who was dying. I found it was a young man referred to on the 24th Jany. He was not able to enter into any conversation with me, all I could do was to direct his mind to the finished work of Christ as having made an atonement for sin, and prayed. He died about 3 hours after I saw him. 10 p.m.

Wednesday 5th February

There are at present three young men in Ward 27 who appear to be in an inquiring state of mind and have expressed to me a desire for conversation on Spiritual Subjects.

Friday 7th February

A young man died last night on Ward 15 who went through an operation last Sunday. He had perfect peace in the atonement of Christ.

Sabbath 9th February

I was asked to visit a dying woman in Ward 6 whom I had seen several times before& had reason to hope she was a Christian. When I approached her bed she held out her hand to me and said, "I'm gane awa hame[79] now. Jesus told me today that he was gone to tak me hame[80]." I asked if she was glad that she was going home. When her face brightened and beamed with joy, "Yes, Yes," she replied "Its grand tae being getting hame."

---

79 'Going away home'
80 'Take me home'

Monday 17th February

Saw a young man in ward 9 whom I have been giving special attention for about a fortnight. Today he was unable to speak to me. So very weak though he appeared to be quite conscious. I prayed with him & when I left it was with the feeling that he would shortly have to render his account to God. I saw him last Friday & thou I endeavoured to press on him the great need of getting his peace made up with God. Yet he seemed to think he would get better.

Tuesday 18th February

I met with a most interesting case in Ward 27. He said he read more since he had come into the Infirmary that he had ever done before and frankly told me that he was anxious about his soul.

Wednesday 19th February

Saw my friend in ward 25 today again who is in an enquiring state. His case seems a little more helpful today. He told me he had been thinking over what I had said to him yesterday, and he thought he saw it a little clearer but could not say he had believed. I found in conversation that he was like many in a similar state, wanting to feel something.

Friday 21st February

Yesterday read and expounded the scriptures in Wards 7-8-12 Today in wards 4-1-16-

Wednesday 26th February

Though nothing of any interest yet I may say it is all interesting work together. What a privilege & honour to be the bearer of glad tidings of Sal. to fallen men and upon the whole the patients are most attentive-

Friday 28th February

Read and prayed in ward 5 -3 – and more or less conversation with patients individually in all the wards I visited – It is pleasing to observe how anxious the patients are generally to Enter into conversation on Spiritual Subjects – even the Roman Catholics, (many of them) desire conversation with me – and are always glad to take a tract.

Sunday 2nd March

I was the whole of this afternoon in the house with two gentlemen from the "Foundries Boys Society"[81] who were visiting the wards with the view of giving a short account of their visit and what they saw in the Infirmary to the children in their meetings, as they are about to make a collection for the same.

Saw a young woman in ward 8 whom I have had special interest in for some time. She told me she was very weak but happy in the Lord. At perfect peace in Christ. When she told me of her hope her face beamed with joy.

Monday 3rd March

Visited the young Irish girl in ward 8 she was very weak and scarcely able to speak to me. But her face which was beaming with the love of Christ told me of the inward joy she was experiencing in her soul. She said that The Saviour would soon come now and take her to himself and she longed to be at rest.

Wednesday 5th March

I often feel solemnized in going through the wards of the hospital. Frequently I am on my way to speak to some poor sufferer whom I have seen perhaps the previous day, and find the bed empty, having died during the interval of my visit. My God give me Grace to be faithful to the dying and suffering in this house –

---

81 This Society was funded 1865 by 4 men in Glasgow to help young boys working in the Iron Foundries and was a forerunner of the Boy's Brigade. See Dorothy Loudon 'The Glasgow Foundry Boys Religious Society.' https://www.ancestry.co.uk/.boar

Friday 7th March

Visited ward 11 with view of seeing a young lad whom I had a conversation with yesterday, and found he was gone, another occupying his bed. When I saw him yesterday he was in deep anxiety about his soul and said that he had slept little for some nights, he was so anxious. I endeavoured to show him the way of Salvation and left him a reading 16th verse of the 3rd chapter of John's Gospel."He died suddenly." Edith Stewart the young woman in ward 8 who is rejoicing in the Lord told me today that she was from Dublin, but had no friends. I remarked that she had found the true friend. Ah yes, she replied, and he is so precious.

Friday 14th March

Saw Edith Stewart in ward 8 today again she is calm and peaceful. Very weak and not able for much conversation. But she said she was happy and had no doubt about her Sal. I learned today from the doctor to whom she had given her whole history, that she had been an unfortunate.[82]

Thursday 20th March

So a patient in word 7 who told me he was a back slider and was very penitent, thou[sic] he was tempted to think the Lord would not receive him. I repeated several passages bearing on his state and he appear[s] to find comfort in them.

Tuesday 25th March

I came across an old fellow in ward 32 who styled himself a free thinker. At one time he had been a bigoted Romanist but now he denounced his church as an imposter and those connected with it as a set of robbers. When I began to read and reason with him on the need of having a Saviour, and to tell him that Christ was the only Saviour of Sinners. He would neither listen nor reason on such a subject.

---

82 This could be an incomplete sentence.

Tuesday 1st April

This is now the 11th day since father's operation he has done very well but this morning he is not so well I do not think there is anything serious.

Friday 11th April

Though it is now 11 days since I have jotted down anything. It is not because I have had nothing to say. Daily I meet with interesting cases some dying and crying for mercy in their last moments, others calmly and peacefully fallen asleep in Jesus –

Wednesday 16th April

I was called upon last night to visit a woman on Ward 10 who was dying and wished to see me. I found she had been in the house for some time, formerly in Ward 6. She asked me if I remembered a patient who died in Ward 6 in such a bed which I did. She told me that it was some words which this woman said on her deathbed that had been the means of her awakening and which had her to seek an interest in the Lord Jesus. And now she said I have perfect peace, and have no doubt that I am safe in Christ but I wanted you just to speak to me about Jesus- Saw her twice again today, read and prayed on my second visit. She is calm & peaceful- resting alone on Christ. I asked her what she was resting on for her Salvation? She replied, "Christ the Rock."

Monday 28th April

I was sent for to see an old man in Ward 9 on Saturday evening, saw him today again but he scarcely knew me. When I asked him however, if he knew the Lord Jesus Christ, he replied, "Oh yes I am trusting in no other save Jesus"

Friday 2nd May

Just come from seeing two men in ward 14 who has just been brought in from the Saracen Foundry[83] dreadfully burned with metal. I had no

---

83 Foundry in Possilpark Glasgow owned by W Macfarlane &Co. in 1879

opportunity in speaking to them as they were being dressed. Gave a tract to the other patients and urged them to put their trust in the Lord Jesus-

Wednesday 7th May

Visited 6 wards and saw an old man in ward 27 who is very ill from the effects of a fractured leg. I spoke to him of the love of Jesus and prayed with him but he appeared quiet and distant and not inclined to conversation - Visited also a young lad in ward 15 who has got his arm taken off, he is very weak but professes to be trusting alone in Jesus.

Friday 9th May

Saw a Mrs Stuart from Motherwell in Ward 8 whom I have frequently visited. Today she was unconscious but evidently had not forgotten some of the precious promises of the lord Jesus. When I first saw her she told me she could not read. I was in the habit of repeating promises to her which she committed to memory and today she kept repeating. 'I will never leave Thee, I will never leave Thee'.

Monday 12thMay

I spoke to a girl in Ward 26 - from the country, and while speaking to her on the need of having our trust in the Lord Jesus .She told me that she had been led to give her heart to Jesus since she came into the Infirmary. Another young woman in ward 18 - I asked her if she was happy she answered yes but I said are you happy in the Lord? She answered yes when [sic]she told me it was two years since she has been brought to the truth at Mr Wilson's meetings in Ceder Ct –

Wednesday 14th May

When visiting in Ward 30 today there was a visitor in from the country seeing her sister who had happened to be there on a previous occasion. When I have read the 14th chap of John and made a few remarks upon it she told me it had been made a blessing and a comfort to her soul.

Thursday 15th May

I saw a man in Ward 12 who was very weak and it was quite evident that his hours were in The Sand Glass.[84] I asked him about his hope when he answered, That he had a good hope as he had always done what was good. Well I said if that is the foundation of your hope, it will not stand the test at the bar of God. I then endeavoured to show him that there was nothing good in us. We were Sinners by nature and Sinners by practise [*sic*] and our only hope of Heaven was Faith in The Lord Jesus who had paid the debt for us by suffering in own room and stead. Alas how often do I meet with such cases. Men dying and hoping for heaven through their good works instead of trusting in the work of Christ –

Friday 17th May

When speaking to an aged man in world 11 who is dying, as I was pointing him to Jesus as the Sav. from sin and death and hell and to make sure that he was trusting in Jesus alone for his salvation, [he] replied that he could not be troubled as he had enough to suffer already, without taking up his mind with these things. I however felt it was my duty to warn him faithfully of the consequences in neglecting The Salvation wrought out by Christ and offered to all men.

Tuesday 20th May

I saw a young man from Kilsyth in Ward 20 who is in an inquiring state of mind. He told me that he had been in a meeting one evening in Kilsyth and he would have given the world to have got out again for he thought the minister spoke only to him, and that he even pointed him out. I showed him that it was the Spirit of God applying the word preached to his heart and conscience and warned him of the danger of stifling these convictions and at once to give himself to Christ.

---

84 Paterson appears to be suggesting that this man's life was slipping away.

Tuesday 27th May

I had a long conversation with the young man referred to above. I found he was like a great many more when awakened to a sense of their need of a Saviour; waiting till he is better and forming resolutions to lead a new life when he gets better. I endeavoured to show him that his doings would never save him. It was the finished work of Christ-.

Tuesday 29th May

I met with two most interesting cases today, one man in Ward 5 - and one in Ward 6 - both in deep anxiety about their soul, and had been they told me for some time –

Friday 6th June

Saw a man in Ward 6 who has been in the house for some time and is always shown an interest in Spiritual things. Today he has been vomiting blood and is very weak evidently drawing near to the end of his journey of life. He expressed to me his confidence in Christ as his Saviour and was quite resigned to the will of God.

Tuesday 10th June

Visited the same man referred to on Friday. Still very weak but I thought him looking better. He said that he knew if he died that he would go to Heaven. I asked him what reason he had to hope that he would be saved. What was the foundation of his hope? He replied his only hope was, "The finished work of Christ."

Thursday 12th June

Visited 6 Wards in the Medical side. Had not much Liberty or comfort in speaking to the people, with the exception of two or three who seemed interested. The others appeared so indifferent in divine things, almost rude, that I felt indignant at the conduct-

Friday 13th June

Had a degree of liberty in speaking to the people concerning their eternal salvation and I trust was enabled through grace to warn faithfully the sinner of his danger at the same time exhibiting the love of God in Christ the Saviour of all who believe.

Tuesday 17th June

Visited two men in Ward 9-one in Ward 27 and found he had died this morning. One in ward 25 one girl in Ward 23- all evidently on the border of Eternity. God give me Grace to hold up Christ and him crucified before the eyes of the dying.

Monday 23rd June

Visited ward 25 yesterday but the young man who I had gone to see died at 4:50. This was 5:30. I have reason to hope however from what he said to me of his faith in The Lord Jesus that he was prepared for the change. My God give me grace to be faithful in winning souls to Christ. Help me hold up Christ before the eyes of the people. "I, if I be lifted up will draw all men unto me."[85]

Thursday 26th June

Visiting in the medical side it is very pleasing to observe that my visits are appreciated by the majority of the people. I seem to feel sometimes overwhelmed when I think of the responsibility in having so many souls to look after especially when one remembers how indifferent many of them are in regard to salvation. God do thou give me grace, make me faithful and wise to win Souls to Jesus

Friday 1st August

Began duty this morning after a month's holiday. The majority of the patients who were in the house when I left have gone out .Some of them have died Now that I enter upon the work of another year my prayer to

---

85 John12:32

God is for grace that I maybe found faithful. God give me strength to do the work and wisdom to win Souls to the Saviour Lord deliver me from doing the work officially.[86]May I do it from love to The Saviour and for Thy Glory, Amen-

Thursday 7th August

Whilst visiting the Wards. I observed several in Ward 5 that require special attention and one in W.10who are not likely to get better. The Lord keep me to set before them the simple plan of Salvation. So that they may believe and be Saved.

Friday 8th August

I thank my God that I have a measure of joy today in commending Christ to the people and had the satisfaction in knowing that there were several whose hearts were comforted with The Truths which I spoke to them. And I have also the Satisfaction and Joy in knowing that God's word shall not return to Him void. Therefore I look to my Heavenly Father for the blessing-

Tuesday 12th August

In ward 22 in the side room I saw a young lad who was converted about 6 years ago. After I had some conversation with him I said (pointing to a young lad in the other bed) here is work for you, Have you told him about The Saviour and how you were brought to The Truth? When I began to speak to him about a soul & it was not long till I saw he was in an anxious state of mind & that his conversations with him had been blessed. I thought if every Christian was to act in the same way with their neighbour the World would soon be converted to God.

---

86 Paterson believed that his appointment was the result of a direct call from God and therefore did not want to fall into the trap of 'simply doing a job.'

Tuesday 19th August

A patient in Ward 14 told me yesterday that he had been led since he came into the Infirmary to think seriously about Religious Matters and believed that the Services in the Chapel had been made a blessing to his Soul he is a Native of Ayrshire and had a Religious training in his youth.

Thursday 21st August

When visiting Ward 7 today a young man who has been in the house for about a week came up to me in the Ward and said, Sir I want you to tell me how I may be Saved? [*sic*]I replied. I would with great pleasure tell him how he might be saved. I sat down beside him and read several of the promises & when I finished he said, "Then am I just to believe."Just to believe on Christ as having suffered and died for you a Sinner. He at once professed to find peace in believing.

Thursday 28th August

When speaking to a patient in Ward 1 – who is dying, and when I urged upon him to accept Christ at once as his Saviour, he said, "I wish I could, but I cannot though it seems plain enough. He knew he was dying, and unprepared to meet God yet he was quite indifferent as to his future state. How true I thought, that as a man lives so he dies. I learned from his wife that he had lived a wicked godless life.

Friday 29th August

Saw the patient in Ward 1 today again he thanked me for my attention to him but there appeared no indication of penitence for his past life. Nor any faith in the Atonement.

Sat. 30th –died this morning.[87]

---

87 Added in at a later date

Saturday 30th August

Sent for to visit a patient in Ward 11 when I reached the house I found he was dead. Saw him several times during the time he was in the Ward but could not say he was the least interested in Divine Things-

Wednesday10th September

Met with a patient in Ward 3 who told me he was sceptical in his views and it was with such that he had always associated with. He was however very free in his conversation and said that he was not satisfied as there was as something within, a Secret Monitor which told them that there was a God. Though he could form no opinion about him. I found however when I brought him into Close Quarters[88] with The Word of God, such as our lost state by nature, the punishment due to Sin hereafter, that he would not on any account believe. After a long talk together we parted very friendly and he requested me not to be long till I would return as he really wished his mind to be set at ease on The Matter.

Monday 15th September

Saw a young man in Ward 1 whom I observed very attentive listening to me when I was speaking to a young lad lying in the next bed. After I was done speaking to James Weir (for that was the young lad's name) I went over to him and inquired what was the matter with him. He was sucking ice and told me he had burst a blood vessel. I began to speak to him of the love of God in Christ and the Plan of Salvation. "Ah," he said, I was brought up in the faith of the Lord Jesus but have been very foolish and have wandered away far away from God." I spoke of the parable of the prodigal son[89] and God the Father's Love in welcoming him back into his arms. When I observed his lip quiver and his eyes fill with tears. After further conversation I promised to call soon again &see him. Trusting that my visit was blessed to him indeed I had the satisfaction that it had been blessed-

---

88 Paterson uses the military language of close combat to describe his approach.
89 Luke 15:11-32

Thursday 18th September

Young man in Ward 13 who has been very regular in attendance for some time with evening service, spoke to me the door and said he would like to have a conversation with me but he did not know what to say.He meant a conversation on Spiritual Things as he had been seriously impressed since he began to attend The services-

Friday 19th September

I had a conversation with the young man in Ward 13-Will Craig he is a Porter. He told me that he had had often deep convictions but used to stifle his convictions by taking drink and plunging deeper into Sin.I had often spoken to him about his Soul's salvation and invited him into family Worship in the evenings. He said that I got him to promise one day that he would attend Worship in the evening ,but he did not fulfil[*sic*] his promise & all that night & next day he felt most miserable and attended Worship the following evening. I read part of the sixth Chap of Matt – and dwelt specially on the 33rd ver. Seek first the Kingdom of God and that Verse and the remarks I made from it was, he said, the turning point in his Spiritual History. He described his struggles with Sin and his feelings towards Sin which were very different now from what they formerly were. Altogether from his experience and what he said would lead me to hope that he is certainly a new creature in Christ Jesus-

Monday 21st September

James Weir (18 years of age)an orphan ,died this morning in Ward 1.I have had many pleasant and I believe profitable conversations with him. One day I said James that's a fine word. "He bore our Sins in his own body on the tree."[90] Where I said, can our Sins be if Jesus bore them. They will, he replied, if we believe in Jesus be on him. Yes I said, James have you believed on Jesus?'Yes', he replied I believe on Jesus as my Saviour. Then I said you will be saved. Yes I believe that Jesus will Save me-

90

Friday 26th September

I was requested to visit patient Ward 25 after conversation with him I was about to engage in prayer and requested a patient who was a Roman Catholic to put down his paper, which he was reading, till I was finished, when he refused to do so and became most insolent to me. I told him that he must conform to the rules of the house. When he told me he would not, as he had got nothing to do with me and my prayers. I reported his conduct to the Janitor who came in at the time which he at once reported to Dr Thomas. The Priest happened to be about the house at the same time who when he was told went at once to Dr Thomas. What passed between then I do not know I was sent for to see Dr Thomas and I fully explained the whole affair to him. I thought him a little lenient towards the Roman Catholic. But said however that he would see that I was not interfered with in my duties .

Thursday 2nd October

Visited Wards 10-11-12-5-6-7-8 in all the Wards most of the patients out of bed. Prayed and conversed with one who is dying in Ward 5- 1 in Ward 6 -1 in Ward 7 and also one young man in Ward11 conversed and prayed with a patient in Ward 24 - also with a patient in ward 32 who has been removed from Ward 25.All the patients seemed grateful for my attention and listened attentively to what I said -

Friday 3rd October

Wards visited 16 - 15 – 14 – 23 – 24 - one patient in Ward 5 -2 visits to a patient in Ward 24 who was in a very anxious state of mind and professed to rest alone on Christ for his Salvation

Saturday 4th October

Visited 3 patients in ward 12 in ward 51 in ward 25 1 in ward 27 an hour and a half in the house

Monday 6th October

Visited Wards 18-17-25-26-28-27-2 patients in Ward 1- Funeral Service at 3 p.m. of a Sorter[91] who died on Friday evening in Ward 24- the result of an accident at Buchanan St. Station. I have never seen a dying Sinner in a more anxious state of mind than he was, and I never heard more anxious prayers offered up. I should say more earnest than those which were offered by him.

Tuesday 7th October

Visited a painful case in Ward 32 - an aged man brought in yesterday who had cut his throat with a razor. Though he was not able to speak to me yet I could see from his signs that he was a penitent seeking Mercy. He listened most attentively to me - may the Lord have Mercy on his Soul-

Friday 10th October

I had much comfort in my Soul Today. In conversing with the people in the various Wards and realised much of The Lord's presence-

Tuesday 14th October

Visited Wards 19-27-28-30-29-13-32- Had much comfort in my work today, and was enabled Specially to speak to the men in Ward 13.They were most attentive while I was speaking. I desire my own Soul to be filled with the love of God, so that I may be able to tell it to others out of a full heart

Wednesday 15th October

Visited 7 Wards and had much comfort in speaking to the people. It is very gratifying to observe the attention of the people, (with few exceptions) when spoken to regarding their Salvation. I desire a greater blessing to my own Soul, and for wisdom to know how to deal with the dying.

91 Mail & Parcel sorter

Friday 17th October

Visited 7 Wards and received blessing to my own soul, while seeking to be a blessing to others. The patients upon the whole respectful and several, I might say, very anxious for conversation -

Wednesday 22nd October

Visited 8 Wards and 3 patients in other Wards. Prayed in several of the Wards and spoke individually to the most of the Protestant Patients on the necessity of Salvation and how to find it-

Friday 24th October

Visited wards 11-12-5-6-7-8-16- When in Ward 12- speaking to an old man, the Scrubber[92] was in the other end of the Ward talking loudly with two Patients. I afterwards passed up and sat down at the bedside of a Patient. When she continued speaking and making a noise by removing a stool, I requested her not to make so much noise. When she in a defiant manner replied that she could not help making a noise as she had her work to do and Mip[93] Reid told her she was not to stop her work for anyone

Saturday 25th October

Visited one patient in Ward 15 - 1 in Ward 24- 1 in Ward 19- 2in Ward 27- 1 in Ward 29- an hour and a half in the House-

Monday 27th October

Visited wards 14-15-23-24-18- 1 patient in Ward 9 at Annual Meeting of Dorcas Society.[94]

Hours spent in the house 4-

---

92 This unfortunate title possibly refers to the ward cleaner.
93 Unsure of the meaning of this apparent title could be Miss ie *Miff*.
94 See https://dorcasgri.worldpress.com

Thursday 30th October

The young man Craig, whom I referred to in page 71- told me today when I visited the Ward, before he was led to the Saviour, that he used to bury his head under the blankets that he might escape my notice. But now there was no one so glad to see me as he was. I had much Liberty in speaking to the other young men in the Ward who listened to me with very great respect

Tuesday 4th November

Visited 7 Wards and one patient in Ward 27- it is very pleasing to observe how attentive the most of the patients are when spoken to regarding their Great Salvation. May ,My God bless the word for His own Glory-

Monday 10th November

William Craig left the hospital on Saturday may he be kept from falling away Now that he has to meet and mingle with those who were formerly his associates in Sin. Mary Paterson a girl whom I saw last night in Ward 22 died shortly after I had seen her. She was quite conscious while I conversed with her and prayed-

Thursday 13th November

Saw an old man in Ward 3 from Paisley who seemed to be in an enquiring state of mind and wept bitterly while I was conversing with him-

Sabbath 16th November

Attendance at service tonight- 39 Patients- 9 Nurses and Matron. The most of the patients most attentive, and several appeared in an interesting state of mind-

Tuesday 18th November

Had conversation with a young man in Ward 19 John Flin a native of Edinburgh. He told me that he had been led to give himself to Christ. Since he came into The Infirmary I asked him what had been the cause of thus leading him to decide for Christ. He said partly his affliction and partly in seeing others Suffering so much, and also what I had spoken to him-

Thursday 20th November

Visited 6 Wards nothing of any consequence or of any interest, with the exception of a poor fellow I saw in Ward 16 and prayed with after conversation with him. He had got crushed between two engines. There is little hope of his recovery. He told me he was a member of Mr Johnson's Church at Springburn.

Friday 21st November

Called 3 times to see The Patient in Ward 16 but he was always sleeping- saw another young man in Ward 24, who has lost an arm, he was very sick and vomiting, so that I merely spoke to him a few words. I met with a Mrs Mackintosh in Ward2 who had been a backslider I observed her for some time back attending family Worship and most attentive. On Sabbath evening last preached from Acts 13-38,39 which she said have been the means of restoring to her the pardon, peace and joy she experienced from first she knew the Lord. She said that she had wished to see me before leaving The Hospital, to tell me that she had been restored to The Joy of her Lord, through the Sermon I preached on Sabbath night-

Monday 24th November

Attendance at Service last night, 40 Patients -2 nurses Mip Wood and Dr Thomas. After which I visited 1Patient in Ward 5 - 1 in Ward 27 – 2 in Ward 29 and 1 in Ward 9 - who is very ill. In course of conversation, he said, "I have no fear of death. I know that Christ died for me. I do not doubt, but that Christ died for you only, it must be a personal thing for myself, for me to know that Christ is my Saviour.

Monday 1st December

Attendance at Service last night - 44 patients - 5 Nurses - and Matron. At the close was requested to visit a Boy in Ward 25 - he was unconscious. The parents were present and I engaged in prayer–

Thursday 4th December

Wards visited 9- 10- 11- 12- 1 -2 – Prayed in ward 10- and in Ward 2 -Met with several interesting cases in going through the wards.

Friday 5th December

Wards Visited 3-4-5-6-7-8-16-Prayed in Ward 3-6-7-andhad specially a most interesting conversation with an old man in Ward 3- who was in a very anxious state of mind. When I was endeavouring to set before him the way of a Sinner's acceptance with God I observed tears flowing freely down his cheeks-

Monday 8th December

Attendance Service last night 44 Patients 5 nurses Mip Read and Matron. Had much Liberty in speaking. The people most attentive-

Came across two very interesting cases and Ward 15 - McPhail (a bottle blower) who told me he had been anxious about his soul for some time another young lad who professes to have found peace about a fortnight ago. Had conversation also with a good old man (aged 81) in Ward 17-Prayed in wards 15-17 and 25-

Tuesday 9th December

Prayed in wards 19-27- 20-18- 13- and had much comfort, and a degree of liberty in conversing with the Patients. The most of them willing to enter freely into Conversation on Religious Subjects-

Wednesday 10th December

Visited 5 Wards. Prayed in ward 29-30- and 16-Had much Liberty in speaking to the people regarding their Salvation-

Thursday 11th December

Prayed in Ward 1-2- 9 - With a Patient in Ward 24- and 20- the Patient in Ward 20, is an old man who cut his throat on Tuesday morning and is dying.

Friday 11th December

Prayed twice with a young man in Ward 24 whose live is fast ebbing. He has never spoken to me except expressed a desire to see me -Visited the Cut Throat case in Ward 20-spoke and prayed with them- read and prayed in Ward 6 and prayed in Ward 8-Visited Wards 3- 4 -5- 6- 7- 8-

Monday 15th December

Attendance at Service last night Patients 30-4 Nurses-2Assistants-and the Matron. Prayed today in Wards-15-23-24-not the liberty in speaking to the Patients that I sometimes enjoy-

Tuesday 16th December

Prayed in Ward 28-27-19-20-Nothing of any consequence. The Patients upon the whole, Glad always to see me. With few exceptions they listen attentively to the words of Eternal Life

Thursday 18th December

Prayed in Wards 9-10-11-1-And with a Patient in Ward 19 and Ward 21-

Friday 19th December

Prayed in Wards 3-4-5-8- The Patient I saw last night in Ward 21 died this morning about ½ past 6 o'clock. The patient in 19 died in about an hour after I saw him. Lord give me grace & strength for my work, help me to be faithful, prayerful and watchful for Souls as one that must give account. How often do I see a patient today and when I go back tomorrow he has gone to render his or her account.

Monday 22nd December

Attendance at Service last night 39 patients-4 Nurses-Mip Wood and Matron. Prayed with a Patient in Side Room of Ward 9- the old man whom I saw on Saturday in Ward 25 died last night-

Tuesday 23rd December

Prayed in Wards 10-18-Had much encouragement in conversing with the Patients and met with several cases of interest -

Wednesday 24th December

Prayed in Ward 32-A Roman Catholic rose and went out [of] the Ward whenI began to pray-Visited aPatient in Ward 1-He is in an interesting state of mind, and from what he said seems a hopeful case of conversion-

Thursday 25th December

Prayed in Wards 9-10- 3-Nothing particular of notice, Seeking to keep before the minds of the people, Christ and Him crucified.

Monday 29th December

Attendance at service last night 37 Patients 7 Nurses and Matron

1880

Thursday 1st January

At the annual meeting of nurses. Visited 1 patient in Ward 27-1 in Ward 28-1 in Ward 29-1 in Ward 16-Hours spent in House 2.

Friday 2nd January

Wards visited 1-2-3-4- 9-10 Prayed in Wards 3-4-9 I have at the beginning of another year to record my gratitude to God for blessings received during the past year. Trusting in my God for the future-

Saturday 3rd January

Visited 1 patient in Ward24-1 in Ward 17-3 In Ward 27-1 in Ward 29-2 in Ward 5-

2 Hours in the House

Sabbath 4th January

Attendance at Service 36 Patients, 6 Nurses, Dr Thomas and Matron-visited 1 patient in Ward 9

Monday 5th January

Wards Visited 5-6-7-8- 11-12-Prayed in Ward 5-7-Visited 2 Patients in Ward 9 and 1- in Ward 10

Tuesday 6th January

Wards visited -16-14-15-23-24-17-18-1 Patient in Ward3-2 in Ward 10-

Wednesday 7th January

Prayed in Ward 20 and visited 7 Wards.

Monday 12th January

Attendance at Service last night 40 Patients, 6 Nurses, Miss Read, Miss McKay & Matron.

Wednesday 14th January

Prayed in Ward 30 and 22 met with 3 Christian women in Ward 30

Thursday 15th January

Prayed Ward 10-11-12-8-Saw young man in Ward11 in a very anxious State of Mind. Another about middle age from Kilsyth. He told me that he had been seriously thinking for some time

Friday 16th January

Prayed in Ward 3-4-5-6-Visited the young man in Ward 11 (Robert Reid) he was much better and told me he had found peace last night and was now happy in the Lord.

Monday 19th January

Attendance it Service last night, patients 43-nurses 6- Matron. Had much Liberty in speaking. The patients very attentive- I was sent for yesterday to a patient to Ward 25- who has been in the house for some time and professed his faith in the Lord Jesus, but wished to see me before he departed this life. He died in the evening. Visited R Reid in ward 11 and found him happy in the Lord and other two patients anxious about the Soul-

Thursday 22nd January

Prayed in Wards 11- 9- 5-14-SawR Reid in Ward 11.He is a little better & at perfect peace. Resting alone on Christ for his Salvation.

Friday 23rd January

Prayed in ward 7-8-Nothing special to remark Patients all glad to see me.

Monday 26th January

Attendance at Church last night Patients 27-Nurses 5-Miss McKie- Dr Thomas-Prayed in Ward 14.Had much pleasant & I believe profitable conversation with many of the patients-

Wednesday 28th January

Had much encouragement in speaking to the patients today. The most of them ready to enter into Religious Conversation & several I believe really enquiring-

Thursday 29th January

Prayed in Ward 10- 11- 12- 16-Saw a young man in Ward 16 who was brought in last week & is dying, but is happy in the Lord I spoke & prayed with him-

Friday 30th January

Prayed in Ward 7-16- 14- and had much Liberty in speaking to the patients regarding their everlasting Salvation-

Monday 2nd February

Attendance at Service last night 36 patients,4Nurses,2Super.and Matron. Prayed in Ward 23-Was enabled through Grace to urge upon the people the necessity of an interest in the Lord Jesus Christ-

Tuesday 3rd February

Prayed in ward 28-23-Saw Mrs Henderson in 23 who is very ill prayed with her. The Dr. is doubtful as to her recovery-

Wednesday 4th February

Prayed in Ward 30-Visited Mrs Henderson in the afternoon but she was sleeping and I had no conversation with her.

Thursday 5th February

Visited Wards – 9-10-11-12-12-1-2-1 Pat.W. 23-Prayed in Ward-9-10-11-1-2-

Friday 6th February

Prayed in Wards 3-4-6-7-8

Monday 9th February

Attendance at service last night- 50 Patients- 6 nurses- Dr Thomas-Prayed in Ward 14 twice-Ward 23-18 –

Wednesday 11th February

Prayed in Ward 14-29-30-5-6- I was very much encouraged with a young man Alex Sloan in Ward 7 he is 22 years of age, married and has 2 children. I asked how he was keeping, when he said, he was a little better & before I spoke again, "but I thank God and now trusting in Jesus" I asked when he had been led to find peace and was there any particular means or portion of Scripture."Oh, he said, it was on Sabbath evening in the Church from the text "Mighty to Save." and when he told me, his heart filled and the tears stood in his eyes."Yes," he said, "I know that whatever Shd (Should) happen to me, Christ is my Saviour."

Friday 13th February

Prayed yesterday in Wards 9-10-11 and today and Wards 1-4-14-

Monday 16th February

Attendance at the Service last night 45 Patients, 6 Nurses, Miss Wood & Matron. Subject "Mighty to Save" the Patients very attentive and I had much Liberty in speaking.

Wednesday 18th February

Prayed in Ward's 32- 1-9-

Thursday 19th February

Prayed in Wards 11-8-5-6-The patients, with few exceptions, always glad to see me indeed some of them weary for my Regular Visit

Friday 20th February

Prayed in Wards 3-4- 23- no particular remarks

Monday 23rd February

Attendance at the service last night 54 Patients 7 Nurses, Miss Reid, Matron Had Liberty and the patients very attentive-

Wednesday 25th February

Prayed in Wards 28-32- my own Soul refreshed in Speaking to the Patients-

Thursday 26th February

Prayed in Wards 10-1-2-Hada most interesting conversation with an old man in Ward 9 who is a member of the Apostolic Church-[95]

Friday 27th February

Prayed in Wards 5-6- 7- 8-Read Scriptures and Prayed in Wards3-4-

Monday 1st March

Attendance at Service last night 36 Patients, 4 Nurses-Prayed in Ward 14 today-

Tuesday 2nd March

Prayed in wards 19-28-1

Wednesday 3rd March

Prayed on wards 29-32-Had Specially a Conversation with a man in 29 who is dying and professed to rest on the finished Work of Christ for his Salvation.

---

95 Catholic Apostolic Church, Catherine Street, Parliamentary Road

Thursday 4th March

Wards visited 1-2-9-10-11-12-Prayed in Wards 10-11- and made 2 visits in Ward 16- saw Patient in Ward 1 on Sabbath evening. I was urging on him the necessity of getting his peace made up with God, when he said, "would I not trouble him as he was so weak."On Monday when he realised that he was dying he might have been heard outside of the Ward crying for mercy, I was told when I visited him again in the evening. But when I saw him then he was too weak to speak with and he died during the night-

Friday 5th March

Read the Scriptures in Ward 3.At the close a Roman Catholic entered into conversation with me and quoted Matt 3-6 as an authority for them to confess their sins to man. I explained the passage and showed that there was only one Mediator between God and Man. He calmed down very soon & seemed anxious to be rid of me altogether

Monday 8th March

Attendance at Service last night 47 Patients-4 nurses and Matron- Mrs Henderson, Evangelist,[96] preached for me, owing to my having a severe cold. The two most hopeful deathbeds of those who died from injuries

received from the explosion at Garngad Road,[97]were John McFadyen and Alexander Rynoch. I never witnessed any on their deathbed in such deep anxiety about their Soul-

Monday 15th March

Attendance at Service last night 40 Patients,3 nurses, Miss Reid & McKie

Thursday 18th March

Nothing of any Consequence to note.

---

96 Lay Preacher
97 Now Royston Road, Glasgow

The work of visiting the Patients from day to day seems very much the same, frequently I meet with cases of interest, of deep interest, at other times, carelessness indifference and death reigns all around. Prayed in wards 10- 7-

Monday 22nd March

Attendance at service last night 41 Patients, 2 Nurses, Matron, Dr Thomas

Tuesday 23rd March

Visited 7 wards, prayed in Wards 18-19- and with an old man in 27- in Side Room who was dying. He was very low, but conscious and heard what I said to him- and expressed his Confidence in the Lord Jesus Christ-

Monday 29th March

Attendance at Service last night 47 Patients,3 Nurses,1Assist- Matron- visited 7 Wards. Had not the liberty and joy in my work that I desire to have. Lord give me the Holy Spirit that I may be filled with love for the Sal. of precious Souls.

Tuesday 30th March

Had more joy in my work today. I feel I must be more in prayer if I am to be more in earnest for the Sal. of Souls. I do long for more real fellowship with my Father who is in heaven-

Thursday 1st April

Visited Wards-3-4-5-6-9-10-11-Prayed in Wards 6-9-10- and was enabled through grace to hold up Jesus Christ and Him Crucified before the eyes of the dying-

Friday 2nd April

Visited wards 12-7-8-16-15-14-2 patients in Ward 18Prayed in Ward 8- and had Conversation with all the patients in each of the Wards-

Monday 5th April

Attendance at Service last night 55 Patients-3 nurses, Matron - I thank God for grace given me and earnestness of Soul in preaching the Gospel of the Grace of God. The people were most attentive & it was evident from their appearance that impressions were made-

Tuesday 6th April

Visited 9 Wards, Prayed in Wards 27-22-29-30-14- I was very much helped in speaking to the Patients and realised much of the Divine Presence. One old man in Ward 29, after I had prayed with him took hold my hand and with tears kissed it again & again-

Wednesday 7th April

Visited 7 Wards. Prayed in Wards 1-3-had a conversation with all the patients in the Wards

Friday 9th April

Visited 7 Wards-and prayed in Wards 6-8-9-10-11- Had a measure of Liberty in conversing with the Patients.

Monday 12th April

Attendance at Service last night 60 Patients-2 Nurses-Matron-Had a degree of liberty and realised the Presence of the Lord-

Tuesday 15th April

Visited 7 Wards and prayed in three of them-Had a most interesting Conversation with a Sailor in Ward 19 Side Room. He appears to be in an inquiring State of Mind; when I quoted the verse, "Come unto me all ye that Labour & are heavy laden and I will give you rest."98 He asked if that meant rest here or here after which I explained to him and also what

---

98 Matthew 11:28,29

was meant by Coming to Christ. He seemed very much interested in what I said to him.

Wednesday 15th April

Visited 7 Wards. Saw an old man in Ward 32 in deep anxiety about his Soul. He asked me if I thought God would accept a misspent life as his life had been spent in entire neglect of God & Salvation-After Reading several passages & expounding them more fully in the Way of Salvation, he seemed more composed-

Friday 16th April

Visited 7 wards, prayed in Wards 3-4-6-16- and had some most interesting Conversations with several of the Patients- was encouraged in knowing that I have been the means of blessing and comfort to some of them-

Monday 19th April

Attendance at Service last night 48 Patients-6 nurses-1 Assistant Matron & Dr Thomas. Visited 7 Wards today prayed in Wards 23-18-

Tuesday 20th April

Visited an old man in Ward 32 who has been deeply penitent for the last three weeks but he does not see how God will Save him when he is only going to seek His mercy through fear of hell. Another great difficulty with him is that he has lived 64 years without God& brought up a large family to the neglect of their Salvation-I endeavoured to show him that God wd. (would) receive all come to Him through faith in Jesus &read, "Him that cometh to me I will in no wise cast out."[99]

99 John 6:37 KJV

Monday 26th April

Attendance at Service last night 47 Patients, 1 Nur.[Nurse],Matron Visited 7Wards today Prayed in Wards 24-18-Had several very interesting Conversations with the Patients

Tuesday 27th April

Visited 6 Wards.Was glad to find the old man I refer to on the 20this much better today in body.He told me the Tract I gave him had been the means of much blessing to hisSoul, he appears to be resting alone on Christ-

Thursday 29th April

Visited 6 wards and was much encouraged with several Patients who seem to be in an inquiring State of Mind

Monday 3rd May

Attendance at service last night Patients 37-Nurses 2- Dr Thomas. Had a measure of Liberty in Speaking -Visited 6 Wards today-

Wednesday 5thMay

Saw W Ferguson whom I mentioned on the 20thApril.He is so much better as to be able to be out of bed. More than the Dr. ever expected-

Monday 11th May

Attendance at the Service last night 39 Pat.-6 Nurses-2Assistants- Matron- Had a degree of Liberty in preaching and the people most attentive-

Monday 17th May

Attendance at the Service last night 47 Patients-4 Nurses- Dr Thomas- Matron and 1House Doctor. I did not feel very comfortable as I had not much Liberty in Preaching. I trust however the Word Spoken was not altogether in Vain-

Wednesday 19th May

Visited 6 Wards and though I have not taken a note or kept a daily journal of my Work it is not for want of cases of interest. As I almost everyday meet with some interesting case-

Friday 21st May

Visited a Patient in Ward 12 who is dying. Saw him last night and though I have often Conversed with him, it was only when conversing with him last night that he professed to enter into light and liberty and peace through faith in Jesus. He rested on John 3:16.This morning he is quite resigned calm and peaceful. Saw another in Ward 5 he listens to all I say but gives me little Satisfaction

Monday 24th May

Attendance at the Service last night 40 Patients, 7 Nurses-2Assist.Matrons-3 H. Drs. The Patients were most attentive and I had a degree of liberty in Speaking

Wednesday 26th May

Visited 6 Wards and prayed in 4 of them after conversing with the Patients. Also saw 2Patients in ward 30-1 in Ward 29- the 1 in ward 29 was not conscious and evidently dying. I prayed with the view that it might be made a blessing to the other patients.

Friday 28th May

Visited 6 Wards and kindly received and listened to by all the classes of patients. Catholic is well as Protestant-Supplied each Ward with a fresh stock of good Reading-

Monday 31st May

Attendance at Service last night upwards of 40 Patients- 7 Nurses- 3 House doctors & Matron. The patients most attentive as they generally are, but the officials seemed to be more than usual, attentive and I was glad to hear from one of the officials today that she had enjoyed the Service immensely-

Tuesday 1st June

Visited 7 wards and endeavoured to press on all I spoke to the great need of an interest in the Lord Jesus, without which there could be no preparation to meet God-

Wednesday 2nd June

Visited 6 Wards. Met with several cases of deep anxiety about their Soul. One poor fellow(specially) in Ward 9 whatever had been his past life he was deeply sensible of his Sinfulness before God and his expressions were deeply penitent, and his prayers earnest for God to have Mercy upon his Soul. I endeavoured in the simplest words to set before him the plan of Salvation, when he seemed a little more composed and expressed his trust in Christ

Thursday 3rdJune

Visited wards 11-12- 5-6-7-8- One visit to a patient in ward 1

Friday 4th June

Visited wards 16-15-14-23-24-26- and 2 Patients in Ward 25-One of them a young man, (railway ticket collector) who met with his accident last Saturday at Bridge St. Station.[100]He seems today to be in a Very Critical State

Monday 7th June

Attendance at Service last night about 50 patients-10 Nurses-4 House Doctors-The Patients most attentive- I had much liberty in Speaking and I enjoyed very much of the Lord's presence

---

100 Opened in 1890 www.scotcities.com>railways>bridgest

Tuesday 8th June

Visited 6 Wards and had interesting Conversations with several of the Patients and I have no doubt profitable

Wednesday 9th June

George Lowe died this morning-Went down to Millport with my wife today.

Friday 11th June

Visited seven Wards today. The Patients upon the whole always glad to see me- several even longing for a visit from me-

Monday 14th June

Attendance at Service last night 39 Patients- 9 Nurses- 6 Doctors & Matron-I had more liberty in preaching than I have realised for a long time in the same place. Felt that God was making the Word powerful from the attention manifested-

Tuesday 15th June

Visited 7 Wards also patient in Ward 12 who is dying, and a young woman in 23 who is seriously ill-

Wednesday 16th June

Visited7 Wards also a Patient in Ward 30- Mrs Lees- she was very ill yesterday, but is much better today-

Thursday 16th June

I was pleased to meet with an old patient in Ward 3 who had been in the same Ward last September when he heard me Preach from the words,

"Why sit we here until we die"[101] He told me it had been the means of his Sal. and he continued ever since to trust in Christ as his Saviour-

Monday 21st June

Attendance at Service last night 30 Patients-7 Nurses-1 Assist.-3 House Doctors- I did not realise so much of the Divine Power as last Sabbath evening Although the Patients were most attentive. Visited 6 Wards 2Patients in Ward 14 who are severely burned. They were most attentive to what I said- Also a Patient in Ward 5 an old man who appears to be dying-

Wednesday 23rd June

Visited 7 Wards Met with 2 very interesting cases in Ward 3 who both profess to find peace by believing in Jesus-One of them was not sure if he was right because even in the midst of his prayers he felt over anxious about his wife and children, how they were to be provided for, which he expressed as a want of faith in his heavenly Father -

Friday 25th June

Visited 7Wards and endeavoured to enter into Conversation with the Patients regarding the Sal. of their Soul. Some of them readily opened their minds and told me their thoughts and difficulties in connexion with the Subject. Others listened to what I said but made no reply, while with others again it was too evident, they cared for none of these things-

Monday 28th June

Attendance at Service last night 5Doctors-10Nurses-Matron and Assistant Matron-upwards of 40 Patients enjoyed the meeting, but did not realise so much of the Lord's presence as I would wish. The Lord give me more grace so that I may be faithful-

101 2 Kings 7:3 KJV

Monday 2nd August

Returned from a month's holiday on Friday night .Preached last night in The Infirmary-Attendance 45 patients-10 Nurses-1Sup.- Matron. I had a degree of liberty in preaching. The patients most attentive- visited eight Wards today-

Tuesday 3rd August

Visited 11 Wards Merely however a passing visit with a view of seeking out bad cases, and giving my special attention to them in the first place-

Wednesday 4th August

Visited 8 wards and a patient in ward 7 who is dying.He has been several months in the House.He has professed his faith in The Lord Jesus and from what he has said to me I have reason to hope he is trusting in the Lord for Salvation –

Thursday 5th August

Saw a Patient in Ward 32 who seems to realise his position as a lost Sinner and in deep anxiety about his Soul but he is tempted to think that he has sinned away his day of Grace and for him there is no Mercy. I endeavoured to show him that there was mercy for the chief of Sinners if they only trusted Christ as the Saviour-

Monday 9th August

Attendance at Service last night 33 Patients-4 Nurses-Miss Potter-The Patients most attentive. Visited 7 Wards Prayed in Wards 15-23-17-The Patients all glad to see me-

Thursday 12th August

Tuesday removing furniture & books into another room- Wed-Replacing books in bookcase- and 5 Wards and 5 on the former day. Today visited 7

Wards. Saw very few of the Patients mostly out of bed, and walking out on the green-

Monday 16th August

Attendance at Service last night, Patients 43-Nurses 5-Matron and 2Assist. Mat- I enjoyed the Service and had a degree of liberty in Speaking for which I thank my God. My prayer to God is that the Word spoken may be blessed in the Conversion of precious Souls-

Tuesday 17th August

Visited 7 Wards had some understanding& I believe profitable conversation with several of the patients. I find that upon the whole they are always glad to see me-

Wednesday 18th August

Visited 7 Wards and was kindly received by the Patients. I endeavoured to keep before their minds the necessity of "Looking to Jesus" for grace and comfort. Was asked last night at 11p.m. to visit James Smith who is dying in Ward 1.Sawhim twice today, he is very weak but expressed his hope alone in Jesus-

Friday 20th August

Visited 7 Wards-In Ward 11 saw one young man who is dying and in a very anxious State of Mind whom I had a long conversation with, also another in the Side Room who appeared to be fast sinking directed him to the Crucified and Risen Saviour, "who is able to save to the uttermost" he seemed to be resting on Jesus-

Monday 23rdAugust

Mr Laing preached for me last night as I was preaching in Linwood Parish Church and walked home in the evening. Visited 6 Wards and saw an accident case in Ward 27- and a man dying in ward 24-

Tuesday 24th August

Visited the Parl[102].-Poorhouse in the morning-Male and female insane Wards-1 patient in Ward 3-1 in Ward 2-Visited also 7 Wards in The Infirmary and had a short Service at a funeral at 1 p.m. I had not the opportunity in speaking with some of the patients as I would have wished going to the Painters being in some of the Wards-

Wednesday 25th August

Visited 8 Wards. Saw a patient in Ward 9 who is dying prayed at his bedside-One in ward 11 also dying had conversation with him and prayed-

Thursday 26th August

Visited 8 Wards today. Saw a patient in Ward 11 who is dying-prayed in Wards-4-5-6-And had interesting conversations with several of the patients-

Friday 27th August

Visited 8 Wards, also one patient in Ward 9-one in Ward 11-one in Ward 16-Visited the Prla-Poorhouse in the afternoon- visited all the wards in the North house- also 2 patients in Ward 3 -1 in Ward 5

Monday 30th August

The Rev. Mr Brunton preached for me last night. Visited 6 Wards and one patient in Ward 24-Prayed in Wards 27-29-30-24-Met with a very interesting case in Ward 30- who is in a very anxious state of mind.. (She is a young woman)

Tuesday 31st August

Visited 5 wards and one patient in Ward 24- one in Ward 15-one in Ward 23-one twice in Ward 11-Was very much cheered and encouraged in

---

102 The Poor House moved from Clyde Street to Parliamentary Road hence various abbreviations Parl. Prla. Par.

conversing with several of the patients-Visited also the Parl.-Poorhouse[103] had Worship in the three female insane Wards. Visited other two Wards and prayed with the patients-

Wednesday 1st September

Visited 6 Ward's in the Medical House. Nothing of any Special importance. the patients upon the whole glad to see me-

Thursday 2nd September

Wards Visited- 5-6-7-8-1 Patient in W. 25- 2 in W. 27- 1 in W.30-1 in W. 29- 1 in W. 21- Visited the female Hospital in Par. Poorhouse-

Friday 3rd September

Wards Visited- 16- 14- 15- 23- 24- 25-Funeral Service at 4 p.m.

Saturday 4th September

Visited1 Patient in Ward 29-1 in Ward 27-1 in Ward 25- Passed through Wards18-17- 19-20- and Ward 10- also the Poorhouse. An hour and a half in the house-

Monday 6th September

Attendance at Service last night about 40 Patients-4 Nurses and Matron-Visited 6 Wards today –

Tuesday 7th September

Visited 7 wards. Visited the City Poorhouse, had worship in the female insane Wards-Visited Ward 3-4-1-7 –

---

103 See footnote 97

Wednesday 8th September

Visited 6 wards in the Medical House. Prayed in the Side Room of Ward1. Prayed inwards 3- 4 -5- 6-

Thursday 9th September

Visited 5 Wards. Prayed in Wards- 12- 7- and with a patient in ward 32- Visited Ward 25 with the view of seeing a patient who I saw yesterday. But he had gone to Render his account to God about half an hour before I called-

Friday 11th September

Visited 7Wards and a Patient in Ward 29-Prayed in wards 16-24-29- The Patients upon the whole glad to see me-Visited the City Poorhouse all the male and female infirm wards- and a Patient in Ward 9-

Monday 14th September

Attendance at Service last night, about 50 patients, 8 nurses, 2Super-Nurses,Matron and four House Doctors. Did not enjoy the Liberty I sometimes felt. Visited 6 Wards-A Patient in 29- 3 in 16-And had Service at a funeral at 4 p.m -..

Tuesday 14th September

Visited 7 Wards- 1 patient in Ward 14- and a private patient in ward 7-

Thursday 16th September

Visited7 Wards on the Medical Side saw a young lad in Ward 5 in an interesting State of Mind. Conversed with the patients and prayed- Prayed also in Wards 11-12-29-

Friday 17th September

Visited 7 Wards in the Surgical Side and 3 patients in Ward 12-Visited the City Poorhouse in the afternoon-

Monday 20th September

Attendance at Service last night, 46 Patients- 5 Nurses-2 Doctors and Matron-Visited 6 Wards today-

Tuesday 21st September

Visited 7 Wards.1 Patient in Side Room of ward 6- whom I was sent for last night. She professes to be at perfect peace in resting alone on Christ for Salvation.2Patients in Ward 16.One an old man happy in the Lord-One in Ward 29 in Side Room, who went through an operation on Saturday, he is evidently dying, and has expressed a desire to see his wife-

Wednesday 22nd September

Visited eight Wards. The patients all glad to see me. Was enabled through grace to set before them the Crucified and Risen Lord and Saviour of all who believe-

Thursday 23rd September

Visited 7 Wards and passed through wards 19-27-25-17-No serious cases today. Visited also a Patient in Ward 6 whom I was sent for to see on Monday evening at her request. She seems peaceful and professes to rest in the finished work of Christ

Friday 24th September

No work. Went up to Edinburgh and brought home my wife who has been there for 3 weeks-

Monday 27th September

Attendance at Service last night, 45 Patients-6 Nurses-2 Super-Nur.-Matron-2 House Doctors- enjoyed the Service very much. Visited 6 Wards today. No bad cases, except in 23 Ward. One woman who is dying. Not conscious to be spoken to -

Monday 4th October

Attendance at Service last night 50 Patients-9 nurses-12 Super-[Superintendant] Nurse - Dr Thomas-The people very attentive, and I had much liberty in speaking-Preached at 7th October in my old Mission[104] in Dobbie's loan-Visited 6 Wards today –

Tuesday 5th October

Visited 7 Wards, had pleasant and I believe profitable conversation with several of the patients. I find always someone or another of an enquiring State of Mind-

Wednesday 6th October

Visited 5 wards. Prayed in wards 7-8-6-Had a most interesting conversation with a Patient in Ward 13 which I have no doubt will prove profitable to all the patients who heard what passed between us.

Thursday 7th October

Visited Wards 1-2-3-4-9-10-32- and one patient in Ward 15 – Nothing of special notice, had interesting conversations with several of the patients-

Monday 11th October

Attendance at Service last night-35 patients-8 Nurses-1Sup. Nu.[superintendent nurse] - and Matron- I enjoyed the Service very much and had a degree of liberty in Speaking. Visited 6 wards and spent about an hour with a Patient in Ward 25- who is dying-

Tuesday 12th October

Visited 7 Wards and one patient in Ward 3- an old man in the Side Room. Saw a young woman who is dying in Ward 8-She was to have been married in about a fortnight. She professed her faith in The Lord Jesus-

---

104 Unsure of this outreach. However there was a Tubeculosis Sanitorium in Dobbies Loan, Parliamentary Rd in 1890

Friday 15th October

Visited 5wards and two patients in Ward 3-2 in Ward1-one of them a Sailor who is without friends & home & evidently dying, he is in an enquiring State of Mind-Visited also 2 Patients in Ward 18-

Monday 18th October

Attendance at Service last night-45 patients- 10 Nurses- Miss Potter- Dr Thomas- I had very much Liberty in speaking last night and enjoyed much of the Lord's presence. Visited 6 Wards and had most interesting conversation with some of the patients-

Tuesday 19th October

Visited 7 Wards and had specially an interesting conversation with a R.C. in Ward 13- after which I prayed-

Friday 22nd October

Visited 6 Wards in the Medical House. A young lad in Ward 7 who professed to be trusting in Christ for his salvation, died yesterday. Visited a girl about 14 years of age in Ward 4 who was dying; it was delightful to hear her expressed her simple trust in the Lord Jesus Christ-

Monday 25th October

Attendance at Service last night-34 Patients-3 Nurses-2 Sup.Nurses and Matron. Visited 5 Wards and was at the Annual Meeting of the "Dorcas Society"-

Tuesday 26th October

Was sent for to visit a patient in Ward 29 last night who was unconscious I spoke to the friends and urged upon them the necessity of having their peace made up with God- at the same time saw an accident that had been brought into Ward 16.-Visited 7 Wards Today

Thursday 28th October

Visited 7 Wards. While the patients upon the whole seem glad to see me yet I could not say I observed any seemingly very anxious regarding their Soul's welfare-

November 1st Monday

Attendance at Service last night 22 Patients-4 Nurses-2 Super.Nur.-2 Doctors and Matron. Not so much Liberty as in the previous Sabbath. Which I believe was partly owing to the small meeting which had the effect of discouraging me. Visited 7 Wards today-

Tuesday 2nd November

Visited 6 Wards and had conversation with several patients in Ward 9- but cannot help feeling sad at the indifference which prevails even with those who are dying-

Wednesday 3rd November

Visited 6 Wards, and the young man in Ward 24 whom I was sent for to talk with last night at 11 p.m. He is sinking rapidly but has professed to be trusting in the Lord Jesus for his Salvation- I quoted John 16 Ver. 3 Chap When I came to 'whosoever' he said, that's me. I am one of the 'whosoever'

Thursday 4th November

Visited 7 Wards in Ward 5 Side Room there is a young man 20 years of age dying whom I saw yesterday-Saw him today again he's very anxious about his soul & earnestly prayed God to renew within him and new heart and a right spirit- when I was praying he followed me and at the end of every sentence uttered Amen-

Friday 5th November

Visit 6 Wards and saw the young man in the Side Room of Ward 5- I knew a great change for the worse, he was sitting in bed with the Testament before him I drew his attention to Romans 5:1 and explained the term 'justified' also read to him the question of the jailer at Philippi and the answer of 'Belief etc.' He read it for himself and then remarked that it was quite plain. 'Do you think,' I said to him, 'that you are resting alone on Christ for your Salvation?'"Oh yes," he replied, "I am trusting in Jesus who was wounded for my transgressions and bruised for my iniquities."-[105]

Monday 8th November

Attendance at Service last night- 47 patients-3Nurses-2Super-nurses- 6 Doctors-Matron. Had a degree of liberty and realised the Divine presence- Visited 7 Wards and 2 patients in Ward 5-2 in 27- and 1 in 24-

Tuesday 9th November

Visited 7 Wards, and one patient in Ward 24- all upon the whole very glad to see me, and had pleasant conversations with nota few of them-

Wednesday 10th November

Visited 6 Wards. 1 Patient twice in Ward 18- whom I was sent for to converse with last night at 10:30 p.m. She is much weaker today also one patient in Ward 19 and 1 in Ward 11-

Monday 15th November

Attendance at Service last night-34 Patients-8 Nurses-3 doctors and Matron-Enjoyed the Service very much, the people apparently attentive and had a degree of liberty –

Wednesday 17th November

Visited 7Wards. Prayed in Wards 9 10 11 12 and 32-Realiseda measure of help in conversing with patients, and was enabled to set before them the way of life, Christ the only Source of all comfort-

105 Isaiah 53:5 KJV

Friday 19th November

Visited seven Wards. Prayed in Wards 15-24-26- nothing of any particular interest to note, always endeavouring by God's grace to Preach Christ to the people and urging upon them their acceptance of him as their Saviour

Monday 22nd November

Attendance at Service last night 28[106] patients- 7 Nurses-1Sup.Nurse and Matron- The people most attentive and I enjoyed it degree of liberty.Visited 6 Wards, nothing of any importance.

Tuesday 23rd November

Visited 7 Wards. When about to visit Dr McKewan's I found him with his students in Ward 22, I turned and went into ward 21- when Dr McKewan followed. Then I went into Ward 29 one was dressing there, waited till he left and prayed. Visited 30 Ward and came back to 22, the Students still there- visited 22 Ward again, the Students still there. When I complained to the Nurse as I thought they were only passing the time with some object of their own in view. At the same time I spoke of reporting it to Dr Thomas-

Wednesday 24th November

Visited 6 Wards-Several patients in Ward 1 very weak-Also a bad case in Side Room of Ward 2-Spoke and prayed with her-

Friday 26th November

Visited 7 Wards-Prayed in Wards-7-14-15 and had interesting conversations with the patients in all the wards.

Monday 29th November

Attendance at Service last night-42 patients-7 nurses-1Super-nurse-Matron and Dr Thomas. Had much liberty and enjoyed very much of the Lord's

---

106 In his original writing Paterson writes '28th'

presence. Visited 6 Wards and spoke to the patients after which I prayed in three of the Wards. Also played with a patient in Ward 1-

Tuesday 30th November

Visited 7 Wards and several Patients in other Wards some of the Patients appear quite indifferent when spoken to regarding their Soul's Salvation- others of an interesting nature, evidently of an enquiring Spirit and glad for me to enter into a conversation with them. Prayed in Wards 20- 14- and in the Side Room of Ward 21-

Thursday 2nd December

Visited 6 Wards in the Medical House. Nothing of any importance. Pleasant and I believe profitable conversation with some, others having no desire or wish that I should trouble them regarding their Soul's Salvation-

Monday 6th December

Attendance at Service last night-50 Patients- 6 Nurses,2 Super.-Nurses and Matron. Enjoyed very much the Lord's presence while preaching. The people most attentive-Visited 8 Wards- and 2 Patients in Ward 16-

Tuesday 14th December

Mr Edgar preached in the Chapel last Sabbath night, and I preached for him at North Woodside Road Mission.[107]Though I have written nothing since the 6th yet I not infrequently meet with encouragement in visiting the Wards. Broken bones and sick bodies are often the means of leading the poor people to consider their ways and give themselves to the Lord Jesus Christ-

Monday 20th December

Attendance at Service last night-53 Patients-14 Nurses-one Super. Nurse-Matron & Dr Thomas-Had a degree of liberty in preaching & the patients

107 Free College Church Mission 329 North Woodside Road

were most attentive. Visited 6 Wards read and prayed with a young lad in 19 who is very ill -

Wednesday 22nd December

Visited 7 Wards and while I had a general conversation with the Patients yet I could not definitely speak of any cases of interest. I often reproach myself in not being more faithful. God give me grace, quicken my own Soul, so that I may have a greater passion for the conversion of Souls-

Thursday 23rd December

Visited 7 Wards had interesting conversation with several of the patients-

Friday 24th December

Visited 6 Wards and was much cheered and encouraged with a degree of liberty in Speaking to the Patients regarding theirSoul's Salvation-

Monday 27th December

Attendance at Service last night-38 patients-9 Nurses-2Sup.Nurses-2 House Doctors-Matron & Dr Thomas. Enjoyed the Service and a degree of liberty in Speaking. Visited 7 Wards today. Met with a young man in Ward 25 who has been brought in the other day. He told me in our conversation that he had been converted about 5 years ago-

Wednesday 29th December

Visited 7Wards in the Medical House. The Patients all glad to see me. Prayed in Wards1-3- and had a personal interview with the Patients at least the Protestants-

Thursday 30th December

Visited 7 Wards- 10- 11- 12- 7- 8- 16-14- and passed through wards 15-23-26-28-25--17 Prayed in Wards 12- 7-8-had pleasant conversations with many of the patients.

1881

Monday 3rd January

Attendance at Service last night-50Patients-10Nurses-2Super.Nurses-4Doctors and Matron. Had a degree of liberty in Preaching and from the attention manifested by the Patients I believe the Word spoken was not without blessing-

Having entered on another year I desire to praise my God for the blessings temporal & Spiritual received that His most bountiful hand during the past year, and I would go forward trusting in my God for the future-

Wednesday 5th January

Visited 6 Wards in the Medical House and prayed inWards 3-4-6-10 after conversing with the patients, prayed also in ward 29-

Thursday 6th January

Visited Ward 12-7-8-16-14-15- also 1 Patient in Ward 26- 1 in Ward 27 Prayed in Wards 12- 16-15- after having conversation with the Patients-

Monday 10th January

Attendance at service last night-40 Patients-6 Nurses-1Sup.Nurse-Matron and Dr Thomas. Was very much helped in Speaking and was entirely delivered from the fear of Man, which often hinders one in receiving the blessing of God- the People most attentive-

Tuesday 11th January

Visited 7 Wards and 2 Patients in Ward 29- and 1 in Ward 27- I was cheered and encouraged in hearing of two of the patients who received the blessing on Sabbath evening-

Thursday 13th January

Visited 6 Wards. When speaking to a patient in ward 11, who is happy in the Lord said, I will be alright up yonder. No cold yonder, no suffering yonder, Glorious hope. Another in Ward 7 said, Ah. I will soon be done with time it will be well with us in eternity.

Monday 17th January

Attendance at Service last night-30 Patients- 1 Nurse-2 Sup. Nurses- Matron. Had a measure of liberty in Preaching, The Patients very attentive-

Wednesday 19th January

Visited 6 Wards and had conversation with the most of the Patients with the view of leading them to put their trust in the Lord Jesus Christ. One young man in Ward 12 is very happy. He told me it had been about 2 years since he knew the Saviour-others again though seemingly dying are quite indifferent and do not at all realise their sad and awful position-

Monday 24th January

Attendance at Service last night-50 patients-3 Nurses-1 Super. Nurse- Matron-The Patients most attentive God grant that it may lead to the conversion of not a few who heard the Word-

Thursday 27th January

The work of one day is very much the same every day. Sick and Suffering ones to be Sympathised with, anxious ones to be pointed to Jesus The Sinners Substitute. Careless ones to be dealt with, with the view of arresting them and leading them to think of their Soul's Salvation

Monday 31st January

Attendance at the Service last night-44 Patients-5 Nurses-2 Super. Nurses- The attendance not quite so large as it is sometimes but I do not remember having enjoyed so much of the Lord's Presence for a long time. The patients were most attentive

Wednesday 3rd February

I Have nothing particular to note still I might say that it is all the work of Interest together the patients upon the whole always glad to see me and listen attentively to what I have to say to them regarding the Souls' Salvation

Monday 7th February

Attendance at Service last night-34 Patients-2Nurses-1Sup. Nurse- Dr Thomas. Subject-"God is Love" I had a measure of liberty from the very nature of the subject. Visited 6 Wards prayed in Ward 17-25- 28-20-

Tuesday 8th February

Visited 7 Wards. In Ward 30I observed a (R C) prayer book on the side table beside a Protestant patient. I asked who was reading this book, when a R.C. Patient replied it belonged to the Ward and she supposed if a Protestant was seen reading it I would consider them perverted, but she would think them converted- and before I had time to say anything she said, I believe I am right& you are wrong, for we cannot yet get to heaven without good works-we must work for heaven-I told that I did not believe in the prayer book when she was seeking to prove from it that we must work if we would win heaven, which put her into a rage. I then endeavoured to convince her from the word of God that we were Justified by Faith and not by Works, when she got into a great Fury & I was obliged to leave her as I was not willing to enter into a controversy.

Wednesday 9th February

Prayed in Wards 1-2- 9- 10- 11- after conversing with the patients. Visited also Wards 15 – 32-

Monday 15th February

Attendance at Church last night 37 Patients- 5 Nurses-2 Doctors-1Sup. Nur.- and Janitor. Subject, "Precious Faith, "The patients upon the whole most attentive and I had a measure of liberty –

Friday 18th February

I have been jotting nothing done during the week, not that I have had nothing of interest, because every day I meet with some case of interest either as an encouragement or a warning to others who put off their Sal. from time to time- then death comes and finds them unprepared-

Monday 21st February

Attendance at service last night- 47 patients-4 Nurses-2 Sup. Nu.- Dr Thomas-The Patients were most attentive, and I have no doubt from the attention given that the World was with power. Visited 7 Wards today and was pleased to hear from a patient in Ward 15-that my sermon had been enjoyed by him-

Friday 25th February

It is drawing near the end of another week. How time flies and how little it is lived to purpose. Oh that grace may be given me to be more honest about my own growth in grace and more faithful and dealing with immortal Souls Oh. for Grace to plead with Sinners to be reconciled to God-

Monday 28th February

Attendance at Service last night- 50 Patients- 7 Nurses-1Sup.Nur.- and Matron. I had a degree of liberty in preaching. 'Subject' "The Glorious Gospel of the Blessed God."

Wednesday 3rd March

Visited 6 Wards I prayed in 4 of the Wards after conversing with the patients. Had a most interesting conversation with some of the Patients especially in Ward 9-

Thursday 4th March

Visited wards 5- 6-7- 8- 16-14 and 2 patients in ward 18-1 in Ward 25-

Friday 5th March

Visited Wards 11- 12-15- 23-24-26-25- visited 1 Patient in Ward 16 1 in Ward 7- nothing particularly to notice, the Patients upon the whole glad to see me-

Monday 7th March

Attendance at Service last night- 52 Patients- 8 Nurses-1Sup. Nurse-Matron- Dr Thomas. Enjoyed the Service very much the Patients very attentive, and judging from their appearance I have no doubt the Word was effectual-

Wednesday 9th March

Nothing of much importance. Just the same thing over again. Sickness, Suffering and death, some of them very sad deaths

Monday 14th March

Attendance at Service last night 60 Patients- 5 Nurses-1 Sup. Nurse &Matron. Enjoyed the Service very much and had liberty in Speaking and commending my Master-

Monday 21st March

I was preaching in Largs U.P. Church[108] yesterday Mr Laing preached for me in the evening-

Tuesday 22nd March

I was about to pray in Ward 2-Some of the patients were in the Side Room and I sent the patient in to tell them to be quiet, Still the noise went on till I had to go in and rebuke them, when the Nurse came out and spoke to them about it-

---

108 United Presbyterian Church, Largs, Ayrshire

Monday 28thMarch

Attendance at Service last night- 40 Patients- 5 Nurses- Matron. I had to shorten the Service, owing to the Chapel not being properly heated up and the Patients were shivering with cold. I enjoyed the Service very much and the Patients were most attentive-

Tuesday 29th March

Saw a most interesting case of a young man in Ward 9 who is very weak and fast sinking. He said to me that he would not like to get better, he would rather go and be with Jesus-

Monday 4th April

Attendance at Service last night about 40 Patients, 5 Nurses,1Sup. Nurse and Matron- I had not the liberty in speaking I sometimes have although the Patients seemed most attentive-

Friday 8thApril

wards visited 16 15 23 24 17-18

Saturday 9thApril

I visited the patient to Mordor level 1 in ward 18 3 in world 25 1 in world 3:27 Ward 17 21 29 hours spent in the House 2

Monday 11th April

Attendance Service last night about 40 Patients,2 Nurses- and Matron-

Thursday 14th April

Visited Wards 12- 7- 8- 16- 14- 15 Visited 2 Patients in Ward 9- also one Patient in ward 12 last night after worship was over-

Monday 18th April

Attendance at Service last night 46 Patients-3 Nurses-Miss Porter and Matron-

Monday 24th April

Attendance at Service last night 40 Patients- 6 nurses- Matron-Was very much helped in Speaking and had a degree of liberty

Tuesday 25th April

In Visiting the Wards today I met with several very interesting cases, and was therefore cheered and refreshed in Spirit-

Thursday 27th April

Visiting Ward 7 - I had conversation with a patient who is dying. He expressed to me his assurance of Salvation in Christ, and was very happy. He told me it was about 9 years since he was Converted and said it was well for him that he had not his peace to make up with God now-

Monday 2nd May

Attendance at Service last night 30 Patients-5 Nurses-3 Doctors-The meeting was small and I had not much liberty when speaking-

Thursday 5th May

Wards Visited – 12--8-16-14-15-23-Very much encouraged in conversing with the patients, several interesting cases-

Monday 9th May

Attendance at Service last night upwards of 50 patients-5 Nurses-1 Super. Nurse & Matron-The Patients most attentive and I had a considerable degree of liberty in speaking-

Monday 16th May

Attendance at Service last night about 40 Patients-4Nurses-2Super. Nurses-4 Doctors & Matron. I did not enjoy the Service so much as I would have wished, but I trust the Word spoken will not be without effect-

Wednesday 18th May

In Ward 6 met with a Servant (an Irish girl) in a very interesting State of Mind who has been anxious for some time -

Monday 23rd May

Attendance of Service last night about 70 Patients- 6 Nurses-Miss Potter-Matron & Dr Thomas-Enjoyed the Meeting very much and had a measure of liberty in Speaking-

Wednesday 25th May

Visited 6 Wards in the Medical Side, Well received and the Patients were upon the whole glad to be spoken to regarding their Sal.

Thursday 26th May

Visited Wards 3- 4- 5- 6- 7- 8-Visited 1 Patient in Ward 16 -1 in Ward 14- 1 in Ward 18-Very much cheered and encouraged in endeavouring to commend Jesus as the Sav. of all who believe-

Monday 30th May

Attendance at Service last night, 40 Patients-1 Sup. Nurse- Dr Thomas-Enjoyed the meeting and had a degree of liberty-

Thursday 2ndJune

Visited Wards 11-12-5-6-7-8- nothing of much interest.Came acrossan enquirerin Ward 6 - A young man in Ward 12 rejoicing in the Lord

Monday 6th June

Mr Laing addressed the Meeting last night- I preached for him in the afternoon- and Mr Fraser in the evening–

Thursday 9th June

Wards Visited 5- 6- 7- 8- 12- 16- 14-Visited 1 Patient in Ward 15- 1 in Ward 28- 1 in Ward 19-

Monday 13th June

Attendance at Service last night- 40 Patients-4 Nurses-2Sup. Nurses-Matron-Enjoyed the Meeting and had a measure of liberty

Monday 20th June

Attendance at Service last night- 34 Patients- 6 Nurses-4 Doctors-Miss Laing- Matron-Did not enjoy the Meeting so much as I sometimes do-

Monday 27thJune

Attendance at Service last night-36 Patients- 5 Nurses-Miss Potter and Dr Thomas. Enjoyed the Service and had a measure of liberty -

Monday 4th July

Attendance at Service last night- 27 Patients-Nurses 7 - 2 Sup. Nurses-Enjoyed my Subject and had a measure of liberty, realised the Divine presence.

Thursday 7th July

Visited Wards 16- 15- 14- 23- 24- 17- 18- 1 Patient in Ward 16

Friday 8th July

Wards visited- 25- 26- 28 -27- 19-20- 1 Patient in Ward 18- 1 in Ward 3 -2 in Ward 5-

Monday 11th July

Attendance at Church last night- 23 Patients- 7 Nurses-1Sup. Nurse-Matron-Enjoyed Meeting very much and realised the Master's presence-

Thursday 14th July

Wards Visited- 16- 15- 14- 23- 25- 18- 17-Had a conversation with an interesting young lad in Ward 17 - he professes to have given himself to Christ before he came into the Infirmary-

Monday 18th July

Attendance at Service last night-33 Patients- 9Nurses- 1 Sup. Nurse-Matron -A very enjoyable meeting and had a degree of liberty in speaking. The Patients most attentive-

Thursday 21st July

Wards visited 18-17-25-26-20-28- The work very pleasant the Patients with few exceptions always ready to hear a word of exhortation. Many of them very grateful for a word of comfort and sympathy. May the Lord stir up my own Soul so that I may be found faithful in the discharge of my duty that I may know nothing but Jesus Christ and him crucified-

Monday 25th July

Attendance at Service last night- 49 Patients- 6 Nurses- 3 House Doctors-and Matron. Had a very pleasant meeting and enjoyed a measure of the Lord's presence and was enabled to plead earnestly with the people who were most attentive. I long for more of the Divine Presence that I may be made the means of blessing to others-

Thursday 28th July

Visited Wards 25- 26- 27-28- 20-19-Made3Visits to a patient in Ward 18-

Monday 1st August

Attendance at Service last night-35 Patients- 3 Nurses- 1 Doctor- Matron- The attendance not quite so good but enjoyed the Masters presence and was very much helped in Speaking-

Monday 8th August

Attendance at Service last night-33 Patients-2 Nurses-1Sup.Nur.-Janitor- and Matron -Enjoyed the meeting and realised much of the Lord's presence

Tuesday 23rd August

I have just returned from a fortnight of a holiday, feeling some what refreshed in body and spirit. I trust that I should be the better fitted for my Work. May God give me Grace to be faithful in the discharge of my duty.

Thursday 21st August

Wards visited 8- 18- 17- 25- 26- 28- 27-Visited 1Patient in Ward 7 –

Monday 29th August

Attendance at Service last night- 28 Patients- 5 Nurses - 1 Sup. Nurse- Dr Thomas. Enjoyed the Meeting but could not say I had much liberty. Enjoyed the Visitation today and had much liberty in Speaking and praying with the patients-

Wednesday 31st August

Visited the Infirm Wards in the City Poorhouse and endeavoured to direct the minds of the old people to Jesus who alone could Save and comfort them-

Thursday 1st September

Wards Visited 25- 26- 28- 27- 19-20-Visited1 Patient in Ward 13- 221/2- Nothing of any importance. The Work pleasant and encouraging, the patients always glad to see me. Some of them so thankful that one feels hopeful that labour for them is not in vain-

Friday 2nd September

Visited all the Male Wards of the Hospital in The City Poor House some of the Patients were very grateful of a visit. Others seemingly indifferent and hardened in Sin-

Monday 5th September

Attendance at Service last night- 27 Patients- 7 Nurses-1 Sup. Nurse - and Matron- had a measure of liberty and enjoyed the Meeting-

Wednesday 7th September

Visited the City Poorhouse. Read and prayed in the Wards of the Female insane. Upon the whole very quiet and attentive-Visited 6 Ward here - 1 Patient in Ward 27- 1 in Ward 5-Both evidently dying-

Thursday 8th September

Visited 7 Wards and had pleasant and I believe profitable conversation with the Patients-Visited Ferguson in Duke St. Prison[109] who has been committed for trial for the murder of his wife. While I was speaking to him he wept and seemed to realise his awful position–

Friday 9th September

Visited the Female Infirm Wards in the Poorhouse after my regular Visitation in the House. The poor old creatures glad to see me-

Monday 12th September

Attendance at the Service last night- 27 Patients-2 Nurses-1Sup.Nurse and Dr Thomas. Enjoyed the Service the Patients very attentive-Visited the Male and Female Hospital in the City Poorhouse-

---

109 See www.theglasgowstory.com

Wednesday 14th September

Visited the Town's Hospital today. Read and prayed in the female Asylum Ward's. Visited a dying man in Ward 3 and another in Ward 5-

Visited 6 Wards in the Infirmary. Saw a poor fellow in Ward 29 who came in yesterday and has had both his legs amputated and yet he seems quite indifferent as to his Spiritual State, and has no desire that I should bring the Subject before him. How different from another in Ward 27 who has lost one leg. Nothing cheers his heart so much as Conversation on the things concerning the Kingdom. He has perfect peace-

Monday 26th September

Attendance at the Service last night,30 patients- 5 Nurses-1Sup.Nurse - Matron- Dr Thomas. Enjoyed the Meeting and had a measure of liberty in preaching. The people most attentive.

Thursday 29th September

Visited Wards 27- 28- 29- 30- 21- 22-22$_{1/2}$ -Visited 1 Patient in Ward 32- who is dying. He has lived a careless life but seems very penitent and professes to be resting on Christ alone for Salvation-

Monday 3rd October

Attendance at the Service last night about 40 Patients- 5 Nurses-1Sup. Nurse-Matron. Had a measure of liberty in Speaking-

Wednesday 5th October

Visited a young man in Ward 19 who had his leg amputated a few weeks ago- he is gradually sinking and poor fellow does not seem to realise his position. I endeavoured to impress upon him his need of a Saviour; he listened to what I said, but got very little satisfaction from him. I finished my Conversation with a short prayer

Monday 10th October

Attendance at Service last night about 40 Patients- 5 Nurses-1Sup.Nurse-Dr Thomas. I did not enjoy the Meeting so much as I did the previous Sabbath, although the patients were up on the whole very attentive-

Monday 31st October

Attendance at Service last night 30 patients- 7 Nurses-1Sup. Nurse- Dr Thomas-had a measure of liberty in Speaking and enjoyed the Masters presence-

Wednesday 2nd November

Visited Wards 17-25- and prayed after conversing with the patients. Ward 19-27-prayed in 27- also Ward 30-32-14- the patients all glad to see me and listen to the words of eternal life-

Monday 7th November

Attendance at Service last night 31 Patients- 5 Nurses-1Sup.Nurse-Matron Enjoyed the Master's presence. The Patients most attentive while I was preaching-

Thursday 10th November

After conversing with the Patients I prayed in wards 2-4-6-7-8-

Friday 11th November

Visited 7 Wards and Prayed in 5 of them- 10-11-12-16-23-The Patients very attentive-

Monday 14th November

Attendance at the Service last night-32 Patients-3 Nurses- Matron-2 House Doctors -Had a measure of liberty and enjoyed the Master's presence. Very much helped in Speaking.

Monday 21st November

Attendance at Service last night- 23 Patients- 5 Nurses-1Sup.Nurse-Matron- I had not much liberty in speaking, did not enjoy the Service as I sometimes do, though the patients seemed very attentive-

Monday 28th November

Attendance at Service last night- 50 patients-9Nurses-1Sup.Nurse-4 House Doctors and Dr Thomas- I had a large degree of liberty in speaking and realised very much of the Lord's presence

Thursday 1st December

Visited wards 9-10-11-12-5-6- read the Scriptures with several with the Patients and prayed in all the Wards-Visited a case of attempted suicide in ward 15 but he was unconscious -Visited a case of accident Ward 27 that came in today, he has lost both of his hands by an explosion -Spoke and prayed with him, he was most attentive. While I was praying I heard him utter a hearty Amen -

CONCLUSION

Little is known about the ministry of Matthew Paterson except that which is revealed in his diary. He seemed to see no significance in the Christian Calendar which was not unusual for a Presbyterian Minister in Scotland at the time. The ethos of Presbyterianism, which was the form of government for the national Church, was clearly Protestant with its roots in the Reformation. The growing hostility between Roman Catholics and Protestants in Glasgow at the time, though muted, was clearly evident in the hospital which makes this diary an important social and historical document in its own right. Certainly there was only an uneasy tolerance between the unnamed Roman Catholic clergy and Paterson who was an authority figure in this hospital.

Paterson's great interest above all others, and a key reason for the tension, was his emphasis on 'saving souls'. The message of the Cross offered a great deal of comfort and strength for those suffering injuries and illnesses where death was often an expected conclusion. The diary reveals the stalking mortality of the time making its way through the wards taking lives daily and in comparison the eternal hope that the message of the gospel gave to those who were perishing - at least to those who were responsive to the message preached and shared. For Paterson, evangelism was the heart of chaplaincy.

The modern Health Care chaplain may find Paterson, with his rather direct approach, professionally unsophisticated, even shocking, and certainly sectarian. Whatever reservations there might be, Paterson was a chaplain who was able to offer a grounded hope in Christ to all those in deep distress and facing an often painful death.

Today, as the very concept of 'spirituality' becomes ever more vague, chaplaincy can easily become merely a listening and reflecting exercise rather than a religious and spiritual ministry. Paterson's diary reminds us that chaplaincy needs spiritual and theological depth as well as personal integrity and is not just the ability to care for people with the 'human voice of reassurance.

POST SCRIPT

I have just returned from a fortnight of a holiday, feeling somewhat refreshed in body and Spirit. I trust that I should be the better fitted for my Work. May God give me Grace to be faithful in the discharge of my duty. (Matthew Paterson 23.8.1881)

This publication, though short, is a significant part of the life of The Royal. It is not a biography, nor does it purport to be so, but it is a richly theological and historical account of the role of a Hospital Chaplain in the late 19th Century.

I am indebted to the Rev Paterson for his reminding me of my 'calling' into pastoral ministry and latterly to Hospital Chaplaincy. As I read and re-read his hand-written account, of the first three years of his ministry, it was my privilege to be privy to his private thoughts; the thoughts of an ordained Christian minister. A perfect example, well no, but I'm sure he would be the first to highlight his failings, real and perceived. But he was an example to me and to any other Christian minister who has responded to the 'call of God' on his life. For some, our role is to offer hope through faith in Jesus Christ and our 'attitudes should be the same as that of Christ Jesus.'

Having recently retired from NHS Hospital Chaplaincy, or more correctly Healthcare Chaplaincy, I am aware of the ongoing discussions and debates about what constitutes the unique core requirement of a Healthcare Chaplain. Patterson would without doubt say, 'Christ!' any other response would be bordering on heresy. But times have changed, following a directive from the Scottish Government in 2002, NHS Chaplaincy provision has moved from Religious observance to a broader definition of Spiritual Care. The vocational call to Hospital Chaplaincy is being replaced by an Academic post grad qualification in Healthcare Chaplaincy. The term Chaplain within the NHS may soon disappear, to be replaced with a more secularly acceptable title of Spiritual Care Provider. Hope for the future based on a Superannuation Scheme rather than a Supernatural God.

Adam Plenderleith